Praise for
*Customize Your Career: How to Develop a Winning Strategy
to Move Up, Move Ahead, or Move On*

"Too often we're so driven by enhancing client relationships and customer satisfaction that we forget to focus on the central figure in all
of it—us! Ms. Usheroff hits the nail on the head with *Customize Your
Career*, providing practical examples and a road map for mastering
the soft skills that differentiate successful business leaders from the
rest of the pack."

—Carol DiSanto
Managing Partner
Director of Client Services
Cline, Davis & Mann

"*Customize Your Career* addresses both the need to look inside yourself to understand the work you should be doing and the savvy
required to find and manage opportunities. Roz's book will be
particularly useful for recent grads and individuals at mid-career or
in transition."

—Karen Hanna
Senior Vice-President of Human Resource Strategy
Torstar Corporation

Customize Your Career

How to Develop a Winning Strategy to Move Up, Move Ahead, or Move On

Roz Usheroff

McGraw-Hill

New York   Chicago   San Francisco   Lisbon
London   Madrid   Mexico City   Milan   New Delhi
San Juan   Seoul   Singapore   Sydney   Toronto

1 2 3 4 5 6 7 8 9 0   DOC/DOC   0 9 8 7 6 5 4 3

ISBN 0-07-142279-X

McGraw-Hill books are available at special quantity discounts to use as premiums and sales promotions, or for use in corporate training programs. For more information, please write to the Director of Special Sales, Professional Publishing, McGraw-Hill, Two Penn Plaza, New York, NY 10121-2298. Or contact your local bookstore.

Selections from "Who Gets Heard and Why" by Deborah Tannen and "How Resilience Works" by Diane Couto, published *Harvard Business Review*, printed with permission from Harvard Business School Publishing.

Unique Ability is a trademark of The Strategic Coach Inc. and used with written permission. All rights reserved. www.strategiccoach.com

 This book is printed on recycled, acid-free paper containing a minimum of 50% recycled, de-inked fiber.

Library of Congress Cataloging-in-Publication Data

Usheroff, Roz.
    Customize your career: how to develop a winning strategy to move up, move ahead, or move on / by Roz Usheroff.
      p. cm.
    ISBN 0-07-142279-X (pbk.: alk. paper)
     1. Career development. 2. Vocational guidance. I. Title.

HF5381.U946   2003
650.1—dc21   2003013016

In Loving Memory of My Husband,
Vincent R. Settineri, 1948–2002

Contents

Foreword   ix

Acknowledgments   xi

Introduction   xiii

Chapter 1   *Your Personal Mission Statement*   1

Chapter 2   *Developing Your Personal Strategy*   19

Chapter 3   *Your Intellectual Property*   35

Chapter 4   *Conveying Confidence and Savvy*   51

Chapter 5   *Mastering the Silent Language*   71

Chapter 6   *Building Your Professional Circle*   91

Chapter 7   *Making Presentations—Connecting
            with Your Audience*   119

Chapter 8   *Gender Talk: Men and Women at Work*   147

Chapter 9   *Developing Your Business Protocol Savvy*   165

Chapter 10 *The New IQ—Your Inspirational Quotient*   185

Epilogue   203

Endnotes   209

Index   211

Foreword

Nido R. Qubein
Chairman
Great Harvest Bread Company
Founder, National Speakers Association Foundation

In the marketplace of life, the seller may set the price, but it is always the buyer who determines the value. Some say value is in the eye of the beholder. Others argue that in the absence of a value interpreter, everything degenerates to price. Ultimately, our primary focus must be on generating and rendering value. When something is personal, it becomes important. Value is always personal, and it is measured by its desirability, utility, and profitability for each of us when we receive it.

If you want to have success and significance—in business and in life—choose to be a person of value! Develop personal power that arms you with the tools necessary to compete and cooperate in our changing world. Every improvement you experience is the result of change. Unfortunately, for the timid, change is frightening, and for the comfortable, change is threatening. For the confident, however, change is opportunity.

This book is all about confidence. Roz Usheroff, my friend and colleague, has assembled between the covers of this resource all the tips and tactics you will need to hone your personal power, increase your value, and achieve your dreams and goals. Over the years, Roz has brilliantly helped thousands of leaders and their teams to grow personally and professionally. Her students always become more productive, more persuasive, and better performers. Roz is the consummate enabler of learning who genuinely cares about her audiences and her readers. Her aim is to nourish the minds of her readers as she nurtures our souls too.

Life is all about choices. We choose to expand our horizons by learning to stretch our wings and attempt new adventures. We choose to invest our time with heroes, models, and mentors who teach us through example. We choose to become better tomorrow than we are today. And now, Roz Usheroff has given us one more wonderful opportunity: to choose achievement over mediocrity, innovation over sameness, education over training, and fulfillment over mere happiness. Read this book to learn. Study it to excel. Refer to it often to stay ahead of the crowd.

Nido R. Qubein is Chairman of Great Harvest Bread Company (200 stores in 38 states) and Founder of the National Speakers Association Foundation. He is an internationally known speaker, author, and consultant. He resides in High Point, NC. You may reach him at nido@nidoqubein.com.

Acknowledgments

As I wrote this book, I discovered as the chapters unfolded that it reflects the contributions of all those people who have touched my life. It could not have been written without the experiences I have shared with devoted friends, loving family, supportive colleagues, and loyal clients. I would be remiss if I did not acknowledge my past and present mentors for championing me to surmount the challenges in my life. I personally thank you, the reader, for your interest in *Customize Your Career*. It is my hope that the contents inspire you to fulfill your dreams and make the world a better place to live in.

I wish to thank my family: Sean Usheroff, my son who has blessed me with devotion and pride; Miriam Gruman, my mother and role model; and Lynn and Eli Uman and family; Shelley and Barry Uman and family; Aunt Lucille and Frank Saladino; and Cousin Lou and Richard DeSimone for their unconditional love and support.

I acknowledge my friends and colleagues, especially Michele and Patrick Bailey, Margie and Ralph Barton, Ruth Berger, Zippy Braun, Liz Cheung, Elaine and Chester Chin, Marion Croft, Cindy Dachuk, Janet and Geoffrey Fear, Jan and Stu Giffin, Mercy and Edward Gilpatric, Karen and Ian Hanna, Bonnie and Terry Jackson, Betty and Frank Lucchese, Jennifer and Rocco Marcello, Sylvia Milne, Cheri and Cy Ostronoff, Marta Pawych, Patty Quinn, Kim Price, Pat Ryan, Kenny Schub, Barb Scollick, Shona Scott, Mae and Art Shievitz, and Harriet Velazquez.

My warmest thanks to Nido Qubein for helping me to define my personal brand; to Peter Urs Bender for being a guiding light in my career; to Jeff Blackman, my personal coach, who inspired me to write this book, and to Dan Sullivan, who made me see that anything is possible.

A special thank-you to Kelli Christiansen, my editor at McGraw-Hill, for her dedication to this book from the very beginning and for championing it every step of the way. Thanks also to Tricia Crisafulli for her dedication, superb talent, and wealth of knowledge. It was she who translated my thoughts and experiences into a compelling message for my readers.

For more information about Roz Usheroff and the programs offered by The Usheroff Institute, Inc., please visit the web site at www.usheroff.com.

Introduction

A STRATEGY FOR UNCERTAIN TIMES

Your company is merging with another firm. Redundant positions are being eliminated. Will you keep your job? Your biggest client is downsizing in a massive cost-cutting effort. As a consultant, will your services be continued?

Corporate employee, executive, or entrepreneur, everyone looks for security in the business world. The problem is that most people look to the wrong places for security, believing that "others" are in control of their destiny. In uncertain times the temptation is to try to "hang on to" the job you've got, to keep your head down while layoffs thin the ranks around you. You hope that your customers and clients see you as valuable, but you want to stay "under the radar" of those who are deciding what positions will be eliminated. Your focus shifts externally, trying to ascertain which way the proverbial wind is blowing. You become caught up in the rumor mill and water-cooler speculation. Your future, you feel, is not yours to decide.

The truth, however, is that in both economic good times and bad, you are your own best asset. You are the human capital that you bring to the table. Whether you are scaling up the next rung of the corporate ladder or leaping off to start your own business, your best tools are your own resources.

By "customizing your career," you personalize your career path with conscious choices and decisions made according to your plan. You can't always have control over business, economic, or life events. However, if you are focused on the type of outcome that you truly desire, you will have a much better chance of achieving it. Throughout the customizing process, you take a step back from the current situation, assess where you are, and decide if changes are necessary. This periodic realignment allows you to chart a course from where you are at the moment to your desired destination. Over the years, your goals may shift and your priorities change. No matter. By customizing your career, you are always at the helm in your journey, following the course or plotting a new one.

Today more than ever, your real power must come from within. To survive and thrive in uncertain business times, you must operate from a position of personal strength—your integrity, your authenticity, your power, and your expertise.

Looking inward instead of focusing externally may be a dramatic shift for many professionals, who have believed that networking and the "power lunch" automatically secured their business futures. Gone are the days when being at the "right places" and dropping the "right names" were the way to get the boss's attention or to impress your customers, however. Window dressing and status consciousness will not get you past the front door of your next appointment. There are no shortcuts to success.

In today's business climate, no one can afford to be a corporate chameleon, trying to change into something—anything—because of what you perceive to be happening. You must be adaptable to be sure. But you cannot mask or undermine the core of who you really are. If you do, you run the risk of professional self-sabotage.

As you customize your career, you will find opportunities to demonstrate leadership and promote your expertise. This will allow you to become more marketable to potential clients and employers. You make a conscious investment in yourself and your reputation not only for the present but also for the future.

On a deeper level, by customizing your career, you are taking responsibility for yourself and your future. You no longer see yourself as a "victim" of economic or business events. Further, you recognize not only the value you bring to the business world but also the meaning and purpose of what you do. You seek to improve all relationships with other people for mutual support and benefit. With this perspective, you gain an inner resolve and a strengthened sense of worth to help sustain you when your professional life is challenged.

The need to customize your career is of critical importance. In today's volatile economic times, less than 10 percent of corporate jobs may be secure. Even if you lose your job or your biggest clients, however, you will not have to start from "square one." Your own recognition of your talents, expertise, and leadership enables you to continually market yourself—and bolster your self-esteem. Thus the loss of a job or consulting contract becomes the door that closes before the proverbial window opens.

The customizing process is based on the principle of authenticity. By this I mean that you must be true to your values, beliefs, and goals. This is the heart of the strategies I have taught to corporate executives, middle managers, and employees over the past 20 years. If you deviate from your authenticity, you may be able to reap short-term rewards, but they will not be truly satisfying. More important, acting falsely or pretending to be something that you're not puts you on very shaky ground. Others will experience you as being less than genuine or, worse yet, untrustworthy. Once lost, a reputation is very hard to regain.

To customize your career effectively, you must become comfortable with self-promotion. This is often a very difficult concept for many people, who don't want to be seen as "schmoozing" to get ahead or trying to make themselves look good. Self-promotion, however, is not about blowing your own horn. True self-promotion is doing what you do best and marketing those skills within your immediate business circle (your customers, colleagues, and senior managers) and within a broader professional circle. Self-promotion is not about standing on a soapbox proclaiming how great you are. Rather, it is a way of thinking about yourself and then acting accordingly. The end result is the opportunity to reap success, live a life of fulfillment, and make a difference to others.

It all begins with a strategic and objective assessment of who you are and what distinguishes you. This is as important for the professional with 20 years or more of experience as it is for the recent college graduate. Marketing one's self does not end when you land a job or the next client. It is an ongoing process that challenges you to let go of the traditional concept of job security. It is no longer enough to believe, "If I do what's expected of me, I'll have a job tomorrow." Even longtime employees, managers, and executives must shed their "entitlement attitudes," meaning, "If I work long hours and do my job, I'm entitled to advancement." Nor can you assume that the clients you have today will automatically be with you tomorrow. Whether employee or outside consultant, you must examine the value-added services that you bring to your company and your clients. You must function like an entrepreneur, constantly marketing yourself and your expertise. Nobody has the luxury of taking his or her employment for granted.

In this book we'll explore several strategies to customize your career. The process begins with a personal mission statement and then moves into action with a strategy to organize and optimize your assets. You will learn how to discover your "intellectual property" of ideas and talents, develop a professional appearance, become fluent in nonverbal communication, enhance interpersonal and communication skills, become more sensitive to gender issues, master business protocol savvy, and inspire others through your leadership.

This technique speaks to all professionals because it encompasses five distinct audiences:

- Corporate executives who seek to distinguish themselves within the company, among colleagues and upper management, and outside the company with customers and industry peers
- Entrepreneurs who constantly market ideas and services but who must not become complacent due to a full workload or pigeonholed because of expertise in one industry
- Employees "in transition" who after several years—often with one employer—suddenly are seeking new jobs

- Senior executives and corporate leaders who seek to encourage their team members to market themselves within the company as well as to clients

- Recent college graduates who must use their education, their eagerness, and their work ethic to distinguish themselves

Chances are you see yourself in one of these segments of the professional population—regardless of your personal circumstances. Perhaps you are looking to make a career change at midlife, or you may be looking to secure your current position. You may be a seasoned professional who continually looks to improve yourself. Or you may be a baby boomer whose plans for early retirement have been dashed by the recent stock market decline.

While today's business world is challenging, your road to success stems from being distinguishable in a competitive business environment. You must become empowered to take charge of your life and your career. With a fuller knowledge of who you are, your strengths and talents, and an appreciation of what you bring to the table, you can devise your plan—to move up, move ahead, or move on.

Your Personal Mission Statement

Picture yourself in the back of a crowded elevator. Just as the doors are closing, two more people squeeze in. You recognize them as people you have dealt with in business (whether you imagine them as colleagues, clients, direct reports, or senior managers). You can see them, but they are not aware that you are there; the elevator is just too crowded. You overhear them as they are discussing you. Now ask yourself: What do you imagine they would say about you?

The conversation that you imagine taps into how you think that others perceive you. Perhaps you assume that your direct reports see you as fair and open to ideas, or maybe they see you as inaccessible. You hope that senior management recognizes your contributions, but you have no way of knowing that for sure. You would like to think that your clients see you as providing a unique service, but you have never discussed this with them. You hope that your peers perceive you as a valuable team member, but you have little interaction with them outside of perfunctory meetings.

Your perceptions—whatever they are—may be 100 percent accurate or completely off the mark. They may reflect your hopes or your deepest fears. Either way, your perceptions of how others perceive you are completely subjective. In fact, because you are perceiving what others' perceptions might be, it is doubly subjective.

Nonetheless, many people allow their "perceptions of perceptions" to drive their behavior, their performance, and even their personalities. They make assumptions, usually inaccurately, about what people think about them, and they make emotionally charged adjustments based on that. As a result, they may underplay, overplay, or project a phony persona. What they are missing is a reality check. Thus they are operating blindly, like driving a car at night with no headlights.

The biggest trap that many of us fall into is that we make assumptions based on how we think others perceive us. This becomes the endless-loop trap; we go in circles without getting anywhere. Like a roller coaster, despite some drama along the way, we come back to the same place.

A far more powerful way to address your "image" is to consider how you want to be perceived. What qualities, talents, and abilities do you possess that others should notice and value? What makes you uniquely you? Today, your real power as a professional must come from within, stemming from your core beliefs and values. This strategy is as important for the seasoned executive who has been around awhile as it is for the entry-level professional. Those entering the workforce obviously do not have years of experience. Nonetheless, they can and must work toward creating a perception based on their intelligence, their willingness to work, their inquisitiveness, and their personal commitment to succeed.

By contrast, consider a group of attorneys I worked with who were in their first year of interning. Their overall experience was one of being intimidated by the senior partners. While they had excelled in the study of law, they had not given much thought to how they wanted to be perceived. They lacked confidence because they did not understand or appreciate their own strengths and values. Instead, they were too shy or awkward to ask questions of the senior partners. In other words, they came from a place of inferiority. They did not seize on this initial opportunity to create a positive impression based on their education and bright, eager minds.

Experienced professionals, including those in the midst of a career change, have the same need to develop and follow an internally focused plan as these young interns. At every stage of your career you must operate from the knowledge of who you are, what your gifts and talents are, and the expertise you have gained over the years. This is the "human capital" that you possess; no one gave it to you, nor can they take it away. It is not enough to get occasional feedback that you are doing a "good job" or meeting certain job requirements. Every day you must measure your own performance—the quality of your work and your interactions with others—to ensure that you are living up to your own standards.

Whether you work for yourself or a corporation, you must operate from the knowledge of who you are and the qualities and talents that you possess. You no longer have the luxury of waiting for the annual review to find out how well you are performing in the eyes of your employer or client. It may be too late.

How can you, then, operate from your personal strength, talents, integrity, and authenticity? The simple rule of thumb is to gauge whatever you do by the measure of the "legacy" you wish to leave behind. Whether you are 25 years old or in your twenty-fifth year of working, the process is the same. Whatever your desired impression—that is, creativity and innovation, leadership, strong interpersonal skills, savvy communications, superb customer service—this desired perception must govern your behavior. You must operate mindful of the legacy that you wish to leave behind—at the end of the day or at the end of your career.

YOUR LEGACY

A few years ago I was asked to put together a program for an exclusive group of sales executives who had been with their company for more than 20 years. They were at the top of their careers. They had achieved recognition for their contributions and had reaped large financial rewards as well. Each had financial assets of more than $1 million. What could I possibly say to motivate these individuals? To prepare for my presentation, I interviewed these star performers. Each of them expressed their gratitude for what they had achieved and now looked for an opportunity to give back. They wanted to ensure that they left behind a legacy when they retired. What good could they do, they wanted to know, in their roles as coaches, mentors, and examples to younger and less experienced sales representatives?

The challenges and opportunities that this elite group embraced are the same ones that you have within your grasp. Regardless of your professional circumstances right now—whether you are in a dead-end job, you have been laid off recently, you are soaring through the corporate ranks, or you have just launched your own company—you are in control of the legacy you leave behind.

> **When we get caught up with the events and activities of our daily lives, we lose sight of our purpose and our goals. Our lives take on more meaning when we know what is deeply important to us and work to fulfill that vision.**

Remember, the impression that you make—in each business encounter, in each client presentation, and even in a casual conversation—lingers long after you have left. This encompasses the essence of who you truly are, how you see yourself, and how you respect and value other people. I was reminded of this one day when I strolled through a cemetery garden.

It was a beautiful fall day, and the leaves were beginning to change. In the center of this cemetery was a patch of grass on which two six-foot granite pillars stood. They were slightly arched toward each other but not touching. They made a powerful statement in their aesthetic beauty. However, there was much more. I was later told that the granite pillars that arched skyward were a memorial left behind by two lovers who had died and were buried beside each other. Their bequest, however, was to create a final resting place for others who had died of AIDS and who could not afford a dignified burial. In this sacred place of comfort was a bronze plaque that read: "Wherever you are, stand in the light."

CHARACTER AND CONTRIBUTION

How you are remembered is based on two things, your character and your contribution as you interact with three key groups of people: family, friends, and business associates. With each group, think about how they experience your "character." This refers to the kind of person you are, your traits, your qualities, your talents, and your personality. Consider the traits and values that are the most important to you—for example, being compassionate, honest, and respectful; having integrity; and so forth. Now, turning to the three groups of individuals, think of how your family, your friends, and your business associates experience you.

Next, define the contributions that you have made (or desire to make) to each group. Put another way, the contribution would be the result of having demonstrated your character. For this exercise, I have shared some of my own personal evaluation, which may be of help to you (see Figure 1-1).

This character/contribution grid is a visual representation of how others experience you. How well you operate from the basis of your

	Character	Contribution
Family	Loving Mother	Champion to my son, Sean, to see that there are no limits to his talents and what he can achieve.
Friends	Compassionate	Someone who responds without first judging.
Business	Great Coach	Inspire others to believe in themselves and to make a difference in their professional lives.

Figure 1-1 Character/contribution grid.

character determines how successful you will be in leaving a legacy. The grid also can be your goal of how you would like others to experience you. For example, if your business character is one of being a "team player," then the contribution you might wish to make is to "work effectively with others to champion and coach," and your contribution might be "to bring out the best in others." Even if you have not yet achieved the level of contribution that you would like, the grid becomes an important tool to help you to determine what you would like the end result to be. This is known as *beginning with the end in mind.*

BEGINNING WITH THE END IN MIND

Most of us do not start our careers with the thought of what others will say at our retirement parties. Nonetheless, this "end" is the goal we must always keep in mind. Stephen Covey, author of *The Seven Habits of Highly Effective People*, says that beginning with the end in mind provides a clear understanding of your destination. It means to know where you are going so that you better understand where you are now and helps you to take steps in the right direction. Moreover, acting with the end in mind gives greater meaning and purpose to what you do each and every day.

Which statement would be more rewarding: "developing my interpersonal skills to become more approachable" or "networking more to get ahead"? While each of us wants to be recognized and rewarded for the job we do, we get greater satisfaction when our job leads to a greater purpose than just our immediate needs.

In these uncertain times, many of us are searching for deeper meaning or purpose in our lives. In our relationships and day-to-day work we are seeking greater connection and satisfaction. We do not want to just "go through the motions" of our lives; we want to feel significant. Because our careers take up so much of our time and energy, it is vitally important to feel that our jobs—how we invest our time, energy, and talent each day—serve some purpose as well.

It might be easier to understand this by appreciating the purpose of others who have "life or death" responsibilities such as trauma center doctors or emergency room nurses. The New York firefighters who rushed into the World Trade Center to rescue others will forever define the term *heroes*. Perhaps your career seems less important by comparison. You may think that what you do does not affect anyone's life. You may even wonder if anyone in your own organization notices what you do. The truth is that your life—professional and personal— is interconnected with others. Your job, your services, and what you do all have a direct impact on the economic system that links us all. Moreover, when you live purposefully and with a commitment to use your time and talent for the best possible outcome, you can truly make a difference in ways in which you may never know.

Consider Judith, who soon after her divorce felt overwhelmed by the sheer magnitude of paperwork that she faced. Personal records, bank accounts, utility bills—everything had to be changed into her maiden name. Each day she would tackle a few of the name changes, an emotionally exhausting process that consumed her time and offended her dignity. Then one day she called the cable television company. Reaching a customer service agent, Judith explained that she was divorced and needed to change the name on her account. Instead of being told that she was "in the wrong department" or would have to "hold," the woman on the other end of the line replied, "I know how difficult this is. I'm divorced, too. I can tell you, things will get better soon." The woman took down Judith's name, verified the account information, and made the changes. Her simple act of human kindness, however, made a profound difference. She had treated Judith with compassion.

DEFINING YOUR PURPOSE

Believing that you can make a difference is a very powerful first step in defining and embracing your purpose. When doing this, however, it is important to focus on your own unique gifts, talents, and experiences. What do you have that can be deployed for the good of others?

At this point you might be wondering, "What does all this have to do with my immediate needs? It's all fine to think about the nice things people will say when I retire, but I have different concerns right now! I'll think about the contribution I can make when I'm in a better financial position." You may need another job right now, or you may need to keep the one you have. Perhaps your number one priority is getting clients for your new business.

As important as those immediate needs are, if you focus only on them and not the proverbial "bigger picture," your successes may be short-lived. If you are consumed with keeping your job and do not consider your long-term role within your department, your company, and your industry, then all too soon you will find yourself right back at the same place—trying to hang on to your job. If you spend all your time and energy trying to "find clients," without considering how your character is experienced by those you come in contact with, then you will soon be looking for new clients.

This perspective requires a fundamental shift in the way we think about ourselves and our careers. This is not about being the fastest rat in the race or the one who knows how to play "the game" better than anyone else. This is about acknowledging and honoring who you really are and your daily contributions. When you operate from this platform of strength, not only will you improve your chances of success, but you also will greatly enhance the happiness you experience along the way.

Keep in mind the wise of words of Helen Keller: "Many persons have the wrong idea of what constitutes true happiness. It is not attained through self-gratification but through fidelity to a worthy purpose."

The above concept is underscored by the findings of Dr. Gerald Kushel, author and motivational speaker, who determined that a truly successful life was one lived with a purpose. While these findings are 12 years old, their validity is timeless. In the September 30, 1991, issue of *Bottom Line Personal*, Dr. Kushel categorized people's lives according to their successful careers, satisfying work, and rich personal lives. He studied 1,200 people—lawyers, artists, salespeople, blue-collar workers, teachers, and students. All had achieved success. Unfortunately, 15 percent of these individuals enjoyed neither their jobs nor their personal lives. The success they enjoyed was only on one level. Of the remaining individuals, 80 percent enjoyed their work, but their personal lives were not satisfying. While they had success and enjoyable work, they were living their lives only on these two levels. Only about 5 percent enjoyed their work *and* their personal lives. This small minority of individuals achieved success on all levels.

Further, Dr. Kushel stated that this small percentage of individuals shared three important traits. The first was an inner peace that allowed them to stay focused. The second trait was definable goals and a sense of purpose that guided their lives. The third was "a sense of adventurousness," which helped them not to take themselves too seriously and provided them with courage to take the needed risks.

These findings highlight the need to find a purpose for what you do. If you only see yourself as a "cog in the wheel" or you work to "pay the mortgage," then no amount of financial reward will make you happy.

YOUR MISSION STATEMENT

From the perspective of your purpose, the impression you want to make, and the end results you wish to achieve for yourself and the greater good, it is time to take the next step. This step is to define and articulate your personal mission statement. This statement—usually no more than one sentence long—embodies your purpose; the deployment of your talent, experience, and abilities; and the end result that you wish to achieve.

Mission statements are common in corporations, stating to employees and customers alike the goals of the company. Rarely do people apply this concept to themselves. Chances are that if you ask someone what his or her personal mission statement is, he or she will respond with a shrug and a blank stare. A personal mission statement, however, is a powerful tool for every professional—whether corporate leader, seasoned professional, or new entrant to the workforce. The mission statement helps you to identify and articulate your beliefs and core values about yourself. This highly personal statement becomes your motivation and the gauge by which you measure your actions, plans, and strategies for the future.

In summary, your mission statement is the result of an internal assessment of who you are and what the unique gifts are that you bring to your organization. As the guide for all your actions and behaviors, your mission statement plays a vital role over time in how others perceive and experience you. In so doing, your mission statement helps you to take actions that define your reputation.

> **What unique gifts and talents do you have? How do you want to use them and for what purposes? These are the key elements of your personal mission statement.**

Consider these three words to help draft your own mission statement: *who, what,* and *how.*

Who. Describe yourself. What talents, gifts, and attributes do you bring to the business world?

What. Outline your goals for the use of those talents, gifts, and attributes.

How. Describe the outcome, including the impact that you want to make and the impression that you want to leave behind. How will you make a difference?

Your personal mission statement might look something like this:

My personal mission statement is to use my leadership and communication skills to help others increase their personal power and elevate their unique talents in the corporate world.

My personal mission statement is to share my wisdom and direction with the highest level of integrity to help people achieve their dreams.

My personal mission statement is to use my leadership abilities to bring about the best in myself and in others and to promote my company and its products.

My personal mission statement is to use my creativity to provide direction to inspire others.

My personal mission statement is to use the written word to instruct, motivate, and support others to achieve greatness.

No one can write your personal mission statement except you. It is important, however, that you delve deeper than your immediate needs as in, "My mission is to earn enough money to pay the mortgage." Nor would you want to stop the process with a task-oriented statement such as "To do what is expected of me so that I keep my job."

While it is important to "do a good job" and to earn a salary to "pay the mortgage," these statements fall far short of your personal power. You have unique talents, gifts, circumstances, life experiences, and qualities. How, then, would you choose to employ them and to what purpose?

THE POWER OF YOUR MISSION

Individuals who know and can articulate their personal mission statements have greater access to their inner resources—their personal power—than those who do not. Put another way, people who have a greater knowledge and understanding of their particular gifts and talents enjoy greater success. They are more resilient when faced with adversity.

I began my business, The Usheroff Institute, a North American communications and image consulting firm, in 1990. One of my first assignments was to work with executives who were in "outplacement," meaning they had lost their jobs in the cutbacks and downsizing that we saw in the late 1980s and early 1990s. Suddenly these long-term employees had to go out and market themselves. It was a real shock to their systems. Frankly, many of them did not remember what it was like to go on a job interview and often resisted the idea of it. They had many years of experience with their employers and a great deal of expertise, and yet it was difficult for them to land the next job.

The reason? They could list their job descriptions and describe what their day-to-day responsibilities had been, but they could not relate it to a bigger context. Despite their years of experience, they could not articulate what they had contributed. Left with only their résumés, they were ill prepared to sell themselves to prospective employers.

Goals for a Legacy of Success

- To be noticed.
- To be remembered.
- To be trusted.
- To be sought out for your expertise.
- To be giving to others.
- To make a difference.

I remember in particular one man who had been an executive for many years at the same company and now was in outplacement. He was gruff and showed by his words and actions that he was highly resistant to the outplacement process. I asked him about his experience in job interviewing thus far.

"The first two times people meet me, they usually don't like me. But by the time I get to the third meeting, they've gotten to know me and what I'm like," he explained.

"But how will you get to that third meeting," I asked him, "if people don't like you the first two times?"

This man's attitude was a defense mechanism to compensate for his fear of rejection. Unconsciously, he made it difficult for people to get to know him. By the third meeting, he let his guard down enough for others to connect with him. The man would have put himself in such a stronger position if he had chosen to operate from the basis of how he wanted to be perceived—as warm and wise.

When you operate from the position of your own personal strength, you become far more marketable—at any age and despite any age—than if you rely on what you think that others expect of you. If you chose to be reactive, you will always be a step behind. Or if you isolate yourself in your own world, only letting your "work" speak for itself, then you may find that everyone has passed you by, and you are left by the wayside.

Tim, an attorney I had worked with through outplacement, had been employed by the same industrial company for 25 years. He was focused and driven yet set in his ways. Those with whom he worked closely genuinely liked him, but he had resisted cultivating a higher profile throughout his career. He had never taken the time—in truth, had never considered it necessary—to contemplate the impression that he made on those outside his immediate circle. Feeling secure in his insular world, he made no effort to build a legacy within the company. This proved to be a professionally fatal mistake.

One day Tim received a dreaded telephone call from company headquarters. In a 10-minute conversation with the new chief financial officer (CFO), whom he had never met, he was told that the company no longer needed his services. After 25 years, his job did not feel like a career to him; it was like a marriage. His termination felt like a divorce with no explanation.

Tim was forced to go on job interviews, something he obviously had not done for 25 years. He was so stiff and anxious in the first interview that he was not seen as a viable candidate—and he knew it. He was all buttoned up in a three-piece suit of armor, trying to play the part that he had all those years. As a result, he projected aloofness and an inability to connect. If, though, he had a personal mission statement, he would have had greater control over other people's experience of him.

Luckily, there are concrete strategies that you can adopt that will help you to take charge of your career, to find greater satisfaction in what you do, and to market yourself with integrity and authenticity. These proactive steps are the culmination of the work I have done over the years with many successful people, who have taken control and broadened the scope of opportunities made available to them.

STEPS TO SUCCESS

- *Mission.* What talents, experience, knowledge, and other gifts do you bring to the business world? How would you deploy them to fulfill your business goals and to promote the greater good? What legacy would you leave behind? Focusing on the perception you want to create—as opposed to reacting to how you think others perceive you—launches you in a new direction.

- *Vision.* What direction are you headed in? Imagine that you have already created the right image and have taken ownership of it. Having clarity of how you come across to others, in business and personally, will help you to distinguish yourself and create the results that you seek. Being confident— knowing that when you walk out of a room you have made the right impression—allows you to leverage your talents for the impact you want. Vision in this context is not necessarily knowing where you will be in 5 years but rather positioning yourself in the right direction.

- *Strategy.* What is your strategy for fulfilling your mission? For example, someone may have great ideas but lack the ability to communicate them with confidence. A fear of public speaking is a common but serious disadvantage in the business world. After all, communication is the gateway to leadership. Thus a strategy may be to enhance your presentation skills. If someone does poorly in meetings because they do not know how to deal effectively with confrontation, then seeking training in conflict management would be an important part of their strategy. Or if someone is always late for meetings, which detracts from being seen as responsible and committed, then a time-management course would help. In summary, your strategy allows you to assess your assets and liabilities.

For example, Anne was very scientific minded. Needless to say, she was brilliant and had many innovative ideas. Part of her job was dealing with government officials to help create relationships that would result in approved funding for research projects. The problem, however, was that Anne was not comfortable with the public persona part of her job. She excelled at the drawing board, but in the cocktail party or the meeting room, she would shrink into the shadows.

As part of her strategy, Anne could have taken one of two courses of action. The first would be to seek coaching on her interpersonal skills to bolster her confidence and ease in those business/social situations. The other alternative would be to gather a team that could do the "selling" while leaving her to be the elder statesperson in the room. Unfortunately, Anne did neither. Ultimately, she was moved out of her position and into a less prestigious role in the company. How different Anne's career path would have been had she taken the steps to honestly evaluate her shortcomings!

- *Time frame.* When you have articulated your mission and you have laid out your strategy, you must set a time frame for what you intend to accomplish. Further, when you create your plan, it must be written down. The act of writing creates an unconscious commitment to yourself. Thus, if you intend to improve your presentation skills by joining the local Toastmasters group, you had better give yourself a time frame in which to act—and put it in writing.

  For example, Theo was a brilliant businessman, but he was not managing to grow his business. He had plenty of ideas and strategies, but he just did not seem to get anywhere with them. "Are they written down?" I asked him. "No, they're all up here," he said, tapping the side of his head. Without a written plan, I told him, it was easy to see why he was going around in circles. Finally, Theo agreed to write down his ideas, strategies, and goals and to assign a time frame to them. The strategy worked! With a more sharply honed focus and a stronger commitment to his vision, Theo made significant progress developing his business.

- *Coaches and mentors.* Everyone needs a coach, and everyone needs a mentor. Coaches are not people who know all the answers but rather are people who champion (and sometimes prod) you into taking the necessary steps to further your career. Your coach should challenge you to stretch yourself and to do what it takes. You may find coaches among your peers or friends. I have learned that the people who work for me have been my greatest coaches. I also have a business coach, who challenges me to move out of my comfort zone.

  Mentors are people who have wisdom that you have not yet acquired. Through their perspective and experience, they have the key that allows you to open the door to greater understanding. Often a mentor is someone you seek out occasionally for his or her advice and expertise. The help a mentor gives may be free, but remember, this assistance is not without obligation—to say "Thank you." Too often we take our mentors for granted, failing to recognize them for what they do in our lives. Curiously, our coaches and our mentors may be telling us the same thing that others who are close to us have been saying for years. However, when it comes from a different source, we tend to listen more.

- *Be memorable.* Always keep in mind the impression that you want to make and the legacy that you want to leave behind. You are noticed when you walk into the room with a confident stride, not a swagger, and you can easily strike up a conversation with anyone. You are noticed when you actively listen in meetings, offer suggestions, ask intelligent questions, and articulate your ideas. You are noticed when your work is a cut above the rest because you have pride in what you are doing and you believe that it makes a difference. You are noticed when you bring out the best in yourself and others.

With this in mind, make the commitment to yourself to operate based on how you want to be perceived—not on fleeting impressions based on hopes and fears. Stating your purpose—how you wish to invest your time and talent—will lead you on a new and empowered path. Having a successful, fulfilling career is not a "prize" to be won or a treasure to be taken from someone else. It begins with you and the acknowledgment that you are your best asset.

Developing Your Personal Strategy

Think of your personal mission statement as your destination. This vision of yourself—encompassing your dreams, your strengths and talents, and how you want to employ them—is where you want to "end up" in your professional journey. Your roadmap to that destination, then, is your personal strategy.

This strategy will be uniquely yours, the result of an honest and objective assessment of your talents and strengths, as well as your shortcomings and areas that you wish to develop further. Like a useful and thorough roadmap, your personal strategy will guide you throughout your journey and offer a point of reference should you get off the track.

YOU ARE THE MESSENGER

Many professionals put the focus on the "bottom line." They want to complete the job, hand in the task, process the paperwork, or close

19

the sale. After all, we live in a results-driven society in which the individual is conditioned to deliver measurable results. What too many people fail to recognize, however, is the importance of their unique and personal role in what they are accomplishing. They think that the power is in what is done as opposed to who is doing it. In other words, they pay attention to the message but ignore the importance of the messenger.

Effective salespeople do understand this concept because their success depends on the relationships they have developed. For example, in the pharmaceutical industry, sales representatives often have no more than 3 minutes in which to sell a drug to a physician. Further, there is an exclusive group of "selective see" doctors who may meet with only a few sales reps per month instead of the dozens seen by other doctors. What determines whom these "selective see" physicians will meet? In addition to the clinical and statistical information they want, the overriding factor is the personal relationship developed over time and with care by the sales reps.

While this may be obvious in a field such as sales, I contend that the importance of the messenger extends to every profession. Whether you are a doctor or an accountant, a lawyer or an engineer, the power of you—the messenger—initially exceeds the message or the work that you are delivering. However, substance must be delivered. When you accomplish this goal, particularly in today's competitive and challenging environment, you will ensure that you are the focus, not merely the product you sell, the service you provide, or the work that you do. This begins your journey to building a credible reputation.

THE LIKEABILITY FACTOR

In discovering your power as the messenger, you will quickly encounter a very important and yet often undervalued factor—*likeability*. This subjective judgment is based, as the word implies, on whether or not someone sees you as "likeable." It is a fact of human nature that we all want to deal with people whom we like and who, we believe, like us. However, when we become overly task-focused, we let our work do the talking for us. We lose the vitally important human touch that is the basis of sound business relationships, as well as the foundation of an environment in which ideas are fostered, exchanged, and agreed on. The likeability factor, as illustrated in Figure 2-1, is a down payment on your success. It increases your odds that errors, misjudgments, or other shortcomings will be more read- ily forgiven and overlooked by others.

Shift your focus from what you do to who you are. It is no longer sufficient to let your work speak for itself, let alone for you. You are your greatest strength and your biggest asset. When you recognize and appreciate your personal power, you will have far greater control over how others per- ceive you.

Likeability not only enhances your ability to work as part of a team, it also helps distinguish you as being approachable. This was the experience of Robert, a manager at a large leisure and travel indus-

---

Terry and Chris are executives at a major corporation. There is an opening for a vice president. Terry and Chris are equally qualified to get the promotion. Senior executives meet to discuss who will get the job.

President: "They both have impressive technical capabilities and proven track records."

Sr VP 1: "Yes, but I prefer Terry, who is friendly and polished. The staff and clients find Terry approachable. At the same time, Terry can project authority."

Sr VP 2: "I would have to agree. Chris tends to have a negative attitude and can be pushy at times. To be honest, I'd be concerned about having Chris deal with our biggest clients."

Who do you think gets the job—and why?

Figure 2-1 Likeability factor: Who gets the job?

try firm, who had to develop his "likeability" in order to move ahead in his professional life.

Robert had a very proper and appropriate outward appearance, but his three-piece suits acted as a barrier. Senior management was pleased with his performance yet concerned about how he affected other people. Content to work on his own, often for hours straight with his door shut, Robert was very productive—but aloof. This prevented him from being an effective manager and corporate leader. Colleagues and staff rarely went out of their way to keep Robert informed. Often he learned about changes in policies, situations, and relationships second hand and frequently was caught off guard.

For many reasons, including his own naturally reserved nature, Robert had put all his focus on what he did. As long as the job was done, done well, and done right, he was happy. But to reach the next level in his career, he needed to work on how he was perceived by others. He accepted my challenge to shift negative perceptions, acknowledging the need to "open up." He took tangible steps to show others that he was truly accessible to them—and to their ideas. He stopped working with his door closed and was pleasantly surprised when colleagues saw the open door as an invitation to connect. He took time each day to walk around the office, to speak with others, and to seek their input.

Did Robert change? Yes and no. He did not go from a reserved individual into a joke-cracking backslapper. Rather, he operated from his authentic self, allowing others to experience the true warmth that he possessed but which he camouflaged from most people. Allowing himself to be more vulnerable, Robert's persona was more attractive.

Robert's success in transforming the way others perceived him was grounded in his own personal mission statement. Committed to the process, he drafted a strategy to accomplish it. Before Robert could take the first step, however, he needed to do his "homework," assessing how he viewed himself and how others perceived him. These two components, which I will discuss in detail in this chapter, will be the foundation of your personal strategy as well:

- *Your internal assessment.* How do you view yourself? Do you see yourself, for example, as naturally outgoing or more reserved? Are you happiest working by yourself or in a group? Are you well organized and methodical, or do you wait to the last minute to prepare because you like "flying by the seat of your pants"?
- *Market research.* How do others see you? If you were to solicit honest feedback from a few key people, what would they say about you?

INTERNAL ASSESSMENT

When it comes to doing an internal assessment, many people have trouble being objective. For example, when I work with clients, I often ask them to write down how they *want* to be perceived. Instead, they usually put down how they think people see them *at the moment.* In other words, they are locked in by their own perception of themselves, for better or worse. When this happens—consciously or unconsciously—they are imposing their self-limiting beliefs on themselves and their performance.

Thus the first challenge is to be introspective. What strengths, talents, personality traits, and style of communication do you have *right now*? Once you have identified these factors, it is relatively easy to move to the next step of devising a strategy.

There are many tools available to help you with your internal assessment, including a battery of personality tests and diagnostics, such as Myers-Briggs Type Indicator. In my consulting, I use diagnostic tools that help clients to see and understand facets of their personalities, particularly as they relate to their work habits and workplace relationships. I have given some fun names to these qualities and traits to provide a better visual picture as you proceed with your internal assessment.

- Cheerleader versus lone gun
- Dominator versus peacemaker

- Trailblazer versus traditionalist
- Wallflower versus live wire
- Wing it versus plan it
- Hermit versus team player
- Reactive versus Teflon

There will be situations where you will demonstrate one of these qualities; that is, you will be a wallflower or a live wire depending on your preferred social style, comfort level, natural personality, and the culture in which you work. Other times you will fall somewhere between the extremes.

Keep in mind that undertaking an internal assessment is like painting a picture. The first step is the whitewashing of the canvas. The first stroke of red stands out until it is blended with the background and another color is added. A dash of black evens out to grays and the subtlest shadows. Think of the colors on that canvas as aspects of your character, blending and contrasting. Together it is a complex and rich portrait, accentuated by a strong brushstroke here and there. Studying the bold and subtle colors, the muted watercolor or the hard edge of an abstract in oil, an image is conveyed. So too with your personality portrait as each facet is assessed, studied, and weighed against the others.

> **Just as a portrait reveals the artist's vision, our internal assessment highlights the strengths, weaknesses, boldness, and subtlety of our personality. No one trait determines who we are any more than a single brushstroke defines the entire painting. It is in the blending and the contrast that the intricacy and depth of the portrait is conveyed.**

Let's take a look at some of the key personality traits as you do your own internal assessment and how each quality typically is displayed in a business environment. You may find that you display behaviors of both category traits, depending on circumstances. However, in order to identify your natural characteristics, remove yourself from stressful situations. Think of how you would more typically act if there were no one to please, nothing to prove, and no pressing deadline to meet.

Cheerleader versus Lone Gun

If you are a lone gun, it is all about the competition—and winning. You are driven to excel, to succeed, and to be noticed. You are probably drawn to professions, such as sales, in which you can really shine, succeeding (or failing) by your own efforts. You bring a vital energy into a group and usually have no difficulty expressing an opinion or an idea. In the extreme, you may be like a "bulldozer" that pushes everything and everybody else out of the way. If you have a strongly lone gun nature, you may find it difficult to manage a group in which you must draw out the contributions of everyone. You believe that your ideas are the only ones that work.

If you are a cheerleader, you are a team player. You are cooperative and sympathetic by nature and easily assume the role of a peacemaker in a group in which there is heated debate or disagreement. You tend to prefer working in teams, where you can use your skills at setting up relationships with others. In the extreme, however, you may be too eager to please and accommodate. Consequently, you have a hard time saying "no" to doing more than your share of work on a group project. Further, when you are confronted by a lone gun in a group situation, as a cheerleader, you are likely to back off from expressing an opinion or to raise another idea.

Dominator versus Peacemaker

If you are a dominator, you thrive on making decisions. You revel in your power to take charge. You often demonstrate macho control behavior and possess high energy. You may run into trouble, however, unless you learn how to manage others without steamrolling over them. You also may have difficulty eliciting feedback, especially from peacemakers, who are put off by your aggressive style.

As a peacemaker, you follow the path of least resistance. You strive to be very tactful and diplomatic. You can be compassionate and a very good listener. You often defer to the group for approval when a decision needs to be made. When you do this, however, you run the risk of being perceived as lacking confidence. You may have difficulty making tough decisions, especially in the face of individuals who are more aggressive and controlling.

The basic commonalities among these first personality types are whether you are an aggressive, take-charge person, or you are more comfortable being part of a collaborative team. If you are strongly one type or the other, you may want to develop other facets of your personality. For example, if you are a lone gun and/or a dominator, you may want to consider developing interpersonal skills, perhaps through a course or workshop, to learn active listening. Your sense of mission and the strength of your convictions are good qualities. Learning to balance them with an ability to encourage and listen to the viewpoints of others is invaluable. If you are a cheerleader and/or a peacemaker, you are probably a valuable asset to any team. But you might want to consider assertiveness training to gain the confidence to express your own ideas and opinions more confidently.

Trailblazer versus Traditionalist

If you are a trailblazer, you love to experiment—not only with the ways of doing things but sometimes with the rules. To you, the status quo is an invitation to try something different. Not surprisingly, you are often most at home in marketing and new product development. Your passion is to move your ideas into action, doing things in a new way. Because you are an innovative thinker, however, you tend to be short-sighted. In your effort to devise a new way of doing things, you may not fully analyze the cause and effect. Your thirst for creative solutions may drive you to bypass needed explanations; you fall short in the step-by-step explanations and, as a result, may be misunderstood.

As a trailblazer, you should not abandon your natural creativity. However, you might seek to balance it with a well-thought-out plan, particularly when presenting ideas to a group.

If you are a traditionalist, you tend to be the repository for how and why things have been done in the past. You not only understand how things are done, but you also see all the pieces that go into a process—including the cause and effect of those individual steps. You are logical as well as analytical. You understand that a change in one area may have a broader impact. The drawback of being too traditionalist, however, is being viewed as resistant to change. You also may be resistant to supporting a trailblazer's ideas, believing that change is not required or healthy. Change for you is often very uncomfortable and can be threatening. Faced with trailblazers, your first thought may be "Why can't they leave well enough alone?"

As a traditionalist, you should not forgo your logical, analytical nature. However, you must be careful not to shut out the ideas of others simply because something "has not been done before." You might actively consider other alternatives.

Wallflower versus Live Wire

As a wallflower, by nature you are reserved, with varying degrees of shyness. You may be warm and charming once you get to know someone or you feel comfortable in a situation. Until then, you may be happiest in the background. As a result, you may have difficulty developing a higher visibility to attract positive attention not just to yourself but also to your ideas, talents, and expertise.

If you are a wallflower, know in advance whom you are going to be meeting so that you can feel better prepared for "small talk" or social interaction. Giving yourself this comfort may help you to overcome your natural shyness to speak with others. Also, know what you have to say. Come prepared with four topics, such as current events, entertainment, sports, and human-interest stories, to help you make conversation with others.

If you are a live wire, being the center of attention is never a problem; it comes as second nature to you. You enjoy and seek out the spotlight. This can become a problem, however, if your outgoing nature becomes a distraction and counterproductive to group efforts or discussions. Wallflowers may see you as pompous and showy.

If you are by nature a live wire, you do not have to abandon your naturally gregarious personality. However, in a group setting, ask yourself periodically if you are the one doing all the talking. Do you draw out comments from others? When they speak, do you listen, or do you "jump in" so that you can say what you want?

Wing It versus Plan It

If you are a wing it type, you are a procrastinator by choice. For example, you may have 4 weeks until you must make an important presentation, but most likely you will wait until the last moment to pull it all together. You are masterful at creativity, innovation, and the ability to think on your feet. You rely on those skills to get you out of a jam when necessary.

The challenge for a wing it type is the long-term project with a group. When faced with several intermediate deadlines that must be met, you will need the discipline to divide the project into a series of tasks. A time-management course may be helpful for you.

If you are a plan it type, you enjoy the process as much as the presentation. With 4 weeks until your presentation, you carefully outline your topic, do thorough research, and write and edit several drafts. You rehearse until the presentation is to your exact standards. Your confidence can be shaken, however, when you are forced into a situation that deprives you of time. As a plan it type, you must be careful not to get too bogged down in the details.

Hermit versus Team Player

If you are a hermit, you are most happy working alone. However, you may find it difficult to delegate or even share tasks to be done when it comes to a group project. You also may be perceived as working in an "ivory tower," creating a barrier between yourself and others. Often your ideas go unnoticed because you fear appearing self-promotional.

If you are a team player, you are energized by others and enjoy working in a group. However, you may be more likely to delay decisions unless the group gives you its blessing. You must be careful, therefore, that you are still seen as a decision maker.

If you are a hermit or a team player, you will always have a preferred working style. However, when the situation calls for a different tactic, be aware of how your particular style affects your work. As a hermit working on a team project, for example, you must take deliberate steps to communicate with and meet with your teammates. Do not just assume that they know what you are doing and vice versa. Conversely, a team player taking on a solo project may need to set deadlines to avoid procrastination. Allow yourself to seek out feedback, but do not get bogged down in looking for everyone else's input and approval.

Reactive versus Teflon

If you are reactive, you tend to be very defensive, ultrasensitive, and emotionally charged—especially when you feel threatened or your stress level is out of control. Other "hot buttons" for you are when you feel overloaded or unjustly criticized. You wear your emotions on your sleeve. You also may be perceived as resistant to change if you react emotionally to it. This could be viewed as an impediment to moving forward. As a reactive type, you may find that physical activity—such as working out or even taking a walk—can help you mitigate your internal stress and provide you with a healthy "time out" from difficult situations. Taking an extra moment to think before you speak, especially if you feel upset or angry, also will help you to avoid saying something that you may very well regret later.

If you are a Teflon type, you roll with the punches. Nothing seems to upset you. Confronted with a stressful situation, you simply move forward and rarely raise a fuss. Being too calm and laid back, however, can project aloofness, boredom, or a lack of drive. (Further, your calm, nondefensive demeanor can make you a target for being manipulated by others if they mistakenly take your calmness for a lack of conviction or "backbone.") If you are a Teflon type, you may want to emphasize your people skills, allowing others to get to know you. Let them know that behind that calm exterior is a sensitive, caring individual.

MARKET RESEARCH

As you develop your personal strategy, I encourage you to solicit the feedback of others. In some companies there are formalized 360-degree feedback programs that seek input from a person's peers, senior management, and direct reports. People from every aspect of contact—thus the 360 degrees of the circle—provide detailed input on how they perceive and interact with that individual. Based on this feedback, a person may find, for example, that direct reports see him or her as involved and actively seeking their input. Peers, on the other hand, may see that individual as self-focused.

As unpleasant as it may be, there are advantages to knowing that not everyone appreciates the value that you bring. Now you have the proof and an incentive to repair misperceptions and unfavorable judgments.

To paraphrase the poet, Robert Burns, it is indeed a gift "to see ourselves as others see us." Seeking feedback from others—peers, direct reports, and senior management—can provide us with valuable insight into how we are perceived.

Even if you do not have access to formal 360-degree feedback, you can still benefit from the perspectives of other people. What you learn may be very surprising. Few of us have an entirely accurate read on how we are perceived. Based on those with whom I have worked over the years, I would say that only 20 percent had an accurate picture, about 60 percent were operating based on at least some inaccurate assumptions, and another 20 percent did not really care how others viewed them.

What too few people realize, however, is that their work alone is not what gets them noticed. Their reputation—how they are perceived—has the biggest impact on whether they are promoted. I can think of several incidents in which a manager who was very good at performing his or her job was not elevated to the next level because of poor "people skills." They were not perceived as being leaders because they failed to attract others to follow them. The unwritten criteria in today's business environment often rest on the question: Do people want to work with you?

People who get promoted are those who are perceived as savvy, confident, and commanding. They have the magnetism and charisma to draw out the talent of others. Confidence will override any lack of technical ability when it comes to assuming a leadership or management role. Technical aspects of a job can be learned; the innate abilities to inspire and lead others are not as easily acquired.

SEEKING FEEDBACK

When it comes to an "external evaluation," you may feel vulnerable. Most of us tend to compare ourselves with others, dealing with our own insecurities about what we lack, especially compared with "other people." Seeking feedback can be difficult because you are not just going to hear how wonderful you are; you probably are going to hear some criticism as well. The good thing is that you will be operating from a position of strength—knowing how you are perceived by others, as opposed to floundering in the dark due to inaccurate assumptions. You may choose to believe it or not.

To begin the process of soliciting 360-degree-type feedback, you need to select individuals who will provide you with honest feedback. In my experience, most people do not want to hurt other people's feelings, and there can be political repercussions as well. Confronting someone with the question of "How do you really see me?" potentially could cause some discomfort for everybody involved. Therefore, it is probably best to explain to others why you are seeking input and what you would like to know.

For example, you might approach a colleague and say something such as, "I'd like to seek out your advice because I respect your opinion. I want to identify how I come across to others so that I can create more meaningful business relationships. What I'd really like to know—not from your own perspective necessarily—is how I come across to other people."

Give this person your permission to deliver honest feedback. You might say something such as, "Is there anything that I need to know? It would really help me to know so that I can adapt my style of delivery or correct any misleading perceptions."

If the response is very generic feedback, ask for more details with a little gentle probing: "How are my actions interpreted when I do that?" or "What is my body language saying?"

Seek out the feedback from your boss or immediate supervisor by requesting a brief meeting with him or her. Explain the purpose of seeking feedback. Your questions to your boss should be more direct. For example: "What qualities do I need to develop in order to move up in the company?"

The same need for feedback holds for the entrepreneur, who needs to know what customers think. Consultants and others who work for themselves do not have the luxury of the guaranteed paycheck at the end of the week. For them, feedback is everything. Being proactive to determine how others perceive you may determine if you retain the client or expand your customer base.

To avoid appearing defensive, maintain calmness in your actions and tone of voice. Write down the feedback that you receive. Show the other person that what they have to say is meaningful.

FIXING A REPUTATION

A reputation is a delicate thing. It takes years to build but can be damaged in an instant. Luckily, your reputation—how others experience and perceive you—can be altered over time, although it is a slow process. You cannot change other people's view of you overnight, and a sudden, dramatic shift in your own behavior will be viewed at the least as temporary and at the worst as suspicious and manipulative. Sometimes a person has to leave a company or change jobs to gain a "fresh start" to rebuild a reputation or to alter false perceptions.

Once you have taken the important steps of your own internal assessment and sought the feedback of others, then you can devise and implement a strategy for your own development. Strategic steps may include pursuit of a higher level of education, such as project management and leadership courses. Your strategy also may include a shift in how you look, such as adopting a more commanding presence to be taken more seriously. You may actively demonstrate greater initiative as a team player or speak up at meetings with greater conviction.

Your strategy puts you in the driver's seat of your future. With a personal mission statement as your destination and your personal strategy as your roadmap, you can point your future in a new direction. The opportunities and possibilities will broaden as you look beyond a narrow, self-imposed scope of limitations to an open vista of all that you are and all that you have the power to be.

Your Intellectual Property

Companies go to great lengths to recognize, promote, and protect their intellectual property. Whether technological expertise, patented processes, or proprietary systems, companies know these are valuable assets. "Intellectual property encompasses the brand name, advancements, technology, and know-how of a company," explained my friend and intellectual property rights attorney Linda Kuczma, who is also a partner with the Chicago law firm Wallenstein & Wagner.

"Intellectual property distinguishes your company's product, whether a commodity product or a new innovation, making it unique in the marketplace. This gives you a distinct competitive advantage that directly translates into increased profitability," she added.

While it may be easy to grasp the importance of intellectual property for companies and multinational corporations, few of us ever stop to think about our own intellectual property. Asked about your intellectual property, you may be hard-pressed to come up with an example. The fact of the matter is that everyone has intellectual property, comprised of innate talents, acquired skills, expertise, and knowledge. Your intellectual property is what has made you successful in the past, and it is what will ensure your success in the future.

The problem for many people, however, is that they do not stop to assess their intellectual property. Asked about their experience or expertise, they will give a recitation of the jobs that they have had most recently or perhaps describe their day-to-day responsibilities. Or they will quote from their most recent evaluation. While these are facts, they only scratch the proverbial surface. Your intellectual property goes far beyond your most recent job description, which list criteria that any number of people could fill. Rather, your intellectual property is what makes you uniquely you. Your natural talents, expertise, and how you have developed them are as important to you and your future as the latest technology is to a cutting-edge firm. In a word, your intellectual property is the *wisdom* that you have gained over the years.

Remember the story of King Solomon. Offered any gift in the world—wealth, property, possessions—Solomon chose wisdom. A very wise choice! Money, material possessions, and even your job can come and go, but your wisdom—the talent you were born with, the experience you have gained, and the skills you have mastered—can never be taken from you. It is deeply engrained in you, like intellectual DNA.

What made you successful in the past will lead to your success in the future. This is the essence of your intellectual property. Rediscovering the talents, expertise, and qualities that made you successful in the past will lead you to a more gratifying future.

FOCUSING ON SUCCESS

Think about your professional past for a moment. What comes to mind? A particular accomplishment? A job done successfully? A project that gave you great pride? Or do you think about a time when you were less than successful, when things did not go your way, or perhaps when you lost that job? Sadly, many people tend to focus far more on what has gone wrong in their lives than on what has gone right. While it is true that you can always learn from your mistakes, there is no educational value in dwelling exclusively on them. The same emptiness applies if you focus on what you do not have or what you perceive as "not happening" in your career. Perhaps you have reached a plateau in your company or industry. Lacking a sense of forward momentum, all you can see is the monotony of the status quo. When this happens, you have been ensnared by the *endless-loop trap* (see Figure 3-1).

Like a perverse merry-go-round, no matter how many cycles it goes through, the endless-loop trap comes back to the place it started. It repeats and repeats, reinforcing the same self-defeating, negative messages: *I can't get ahead. I'm off the fast track. I don't know where I'm heading. Everyone else is passing me by. I don't have my degree, etc. etc.* The endless-loop trap locks you into old patterns, making you sluggish and challenging your confidence. You feel increasingly frustrated and unappreciated. When you begin to lose your enthusiasm, whatever goals you had seem less and less attainable.

There is only one way to break the hold of the endless-loop trap. You must go back in time and focus on specific situations where you felt successful. Acknowledging your past successes will help you to regain your hold on what made them possible—your intellectual property. This, in turn, gives you the confidence to move forward again, to get back on track.

Figure 3-1　The endless-loop trap.

To rediscover your intellectual property, think about three successes in your life, whether professional or personal. What accomplishments, projects, or events do you recall with pride? Go all the way back to your college years and move forward in time. What events stand out in your mind? Write down each of these successes. As you recall these past successes, consider what talents or abilities you exhibited at the time. What skills, traits, and expertise contributed directly to these successes?

Digging deeper, consider what skills and qualities you *know* you possess. This is the innate, natural talent that you demonstrate with ease. You may be using this talent in your current professional role. Or it may be a trait that you have but are not using to any great extent—if at all.

Further, what skills or talents have others complimented you on? If nothing comes to mind, ask close associates this simple question: "If you started your own company tomorrow, what position would you give me?" Then delve more deeply and ask them why. In addition, ask friends what specific advice they would call you for. Then, ask them why. Their replies will give you greater insight into the talents and expertise that others recognize in you. As illustrated in Figure 3-2, as you analyze this feedback from friends and colleagues, along with your own assessment of what you do best, look for the common thread. This thread will lead you directly to discovering your intellectual property.

DOING WHAT COMES NATURALLY

Dan Sullivan, founder of The Strategic Coach, Inc., believes that the talents and skills you possess fall into four categories. The first is what he calls your "unique ability," an innate set of abilities that you were born with and that give you energy. The second are your "excellent abilities," which you have perfected over the years due to experience, education, and repetition. The third are your "competent abilities," with which you can get by but without distinction. The fourth are your "incompetent abilities," which are a source of frustration and distraction and should be delegated.

- What areas and/or tasks provide you with a deep sense of self-satisfaction?

- Consider the skills that you have found effortless to attain.

- Look for moments of excellence.

- Watch for behavior "flows"—when performance is "natural."

- Recall times when you felt energized while engaged in an activity or project.

- Consider the skills that sharpen the more you use them.

Figure 3-2   Identifying your strengths and weaknesses.

Your greatest source of success is what brings you the most satisfaction, joy, or intrinsic pleasure. Dan Sullivan believes that we each possess natural talents that we were born with. Our aim, he states, must be to identify our "unique ability" and to find opportunities to use it fully. Over time, other activities should be delegated to a team of people who each have their own complementary unique abilities.

Chris was in charge of international sales for a Fortune 100 technology company. He flew all over the world to meet with customers. His interpersonal skills were his greatest strength, a talent that came naturally. The ability to connect with people on any level and from any culture was the foundation of his intellectual property. Relying on it, he knew instinctively how to build relationships and satisfy customers' needs. In return, customers were loyal to him beyond the norm. He was often treated as an extended member of the family.

His success caught the attention of a new corporate president, who made him an offer that he *had* to refuse. The new position had power, prestige, and a coveted corner office, but it had no customer contact. Fortunately, Chris turned down the opportunity, recognizing that it would distance him from the unique ability that made him most successful.

In a diverse and vibrant business environment, talents and abilities vary from person to person. The discovery of your talents and abilities allows you to rely on your strength instead of compensating for your weaknesses.

Unfortunately, the traditional corporate world puts an inordinate amount of focus on average abilities—instead of emphasizing each person's unique ability. In an effort to develop "well-rounded individuals," corporations often push to have employees develop greater proficiency in areas where they are the weakest. While this may sound like a good idea, the problem arises when it takes attention and emphasis away from your unique ability. After all, would you have expected Mozart to forgo music in favor of greater proficiency in accounting? Similarly, you cannot lose sight of your true genius just because your career development plan identifies an area of weakness. You cannot become distracted from your source of true talent. If you do, you put your career path in jeopardy. You are setting yourself up to become mediocre.

Barbara was a born salesperson who excelled as a top-performing outside sales rep for a Fortune 100 company. Recognizing her performance and contribution, the company invited Barbara and a select group of other top sales professionals to a 5-day management course. The company's rationale was a desire to harness this talent and motivational force. What the top executive team did not fully grasp, however, was that Barbara's success stemmed from her true talent as a salesperson and her natural inclination as a self-starter. For her, being responsible for and managing others was not a true talent or even an excellent ability. Thus the move out of sales into a management position was not only an unnatural fit from the perspective of Barbara's true talent; it actually removed her from the career path of success.

When you move away from the core of your intellectual property, you set yourself up for failure.

If a new job or promotion does not tap into what you do best and what comes naturally, then it will never be a source of satisfaction or an opportunity to excel. Rather, it will become a constant uphill challenge that will undermine your confidence. You will diminish your ability to distinguish yourself as an expert.

DEVELOPING A REPUTATION AS AN EXPERT

Showcasing your true talent allows you to shine in those areas in which you excel. To do this effectively, however, you will have to let go of those areas in which you do not have a natural gift, inclination, or any true competence. In other words, where possible, you should delegate or negotiate. The truth is, as much as you may dislike some tasks, you may find delegating to be a challenge. Perhaps you are uncomfortable asking others for assistance or admitting that you are less competent in a certain area. Or you may not want to let go of some of the work (and therefore have to share the credit). Hanging on to those tasks that are not among your true talents and excellent abilities may backfire on you. It will dilute your expertise, and it may seriously delay or derail your efforts—and could even sabotage future career opportunities.

Marie had developed a reputation in her company in the early days of the Internet as an expert in Web site development. It appealed to her naturally innovative sense, and she was excited about the prospect of using her talent and interest to make the company's Web site more dynamic. Her boss, however, was very conventional. He was uncomfortable with too much change. He resisted Marie's desire to leap into a new area. Her frustration grew to the point where she went to work for another company with the promise of being able to use her innovativeness. Unfortunately, that opportunity never really got off the ground. The development of the new marketing Web site and strategy was delayed internally by a lack of vision and commitment from Marie's new boss.

Marie kept her focus on her true talent and her heart's desire. Because she had developed a reputation as an expert with her previous employer, it was not long before she was offered her old job back. Her previous boss had moved on to another company, and now the way was clear for her to capitalize on her true talent and passion.

A common complaint from many people is that they do not see any real opportunities to become experts in their current jobs. No one calls on them for their expertise or input. Does this sound familiar to you? If so, could the problem be that you are waiting for someone else to seek you out? Have you made the investment to demonstrate your talent? Do not wait for someone to ask you; offer it freely. You will be surprised at how eagerly your offer will be accepted when you share it. Your reputation will be further enhanced by this expertise and your willingness to offer it to others, as illustrated in Figure 3-3.

Even true leaders are not capable of doing everything themselves. Think of respected government leaders. No matter how intelligent, well informed, and decisive they are, they must surround themselves with advisors to whom they can delegate responsibility. A true leader, in fact, knows how to recognize and develop the talents of others and to get work done through others.

By learning to delegate, you can remove one of the roadblocks that stands between you and your desire to focus on your true talent. This clears the debris that clouds your vision of where you want to go and how you want to be perceived.

Although William had risen through the ranks to become president of the company, he was not good at day-to-day management of people. Luckily for him, he recognized this weakness. His true talent was his innate ability to assess the personalities and attributes of his executive team. Thus he could combine the right personality pro-

- Look for opportunities to be seen, heard, and appreciated.

- Offer advice to those who can benefit from your expertise.

- Speak up in meetings. Let others know what you're capable of achieving.

- Use examples from successful projects that you've worked on to highlight points and to get others to recognize your involvement.

- Promote others' talents; they'll do the same for you!

- Volunteer to chair a project team that requires expertise in your specialty.

- Nurture relationships with high-profile colleagues to learn how they have promoted their intellectual property.

Figure 3-3 Becoming an expert.

file and talents to cover all the bases. These talented individuals were natural self-starters who were able to take on a great deal of responsibility and manage the people side of the business. From his post as president, William was able to capitalize on his strengths and focus on the "big picture" to move the company forward.

SWITCHING TRACKS

As you remove the roadblocks that stand in the way of a more successful and satisfying professional life, you may be confronted with a very large and intimidating obstacle—that is, the fear of admitting that you are on the wrong professional path. Perhaps you have been drifting along on the current of least resistance through your career until now. Job changes, promotions, and lateral moves were made on the basis of opportunities that came to you or because the company decided to place you elsewhere. Perhaps you became an independent contractor as an extension of previous jobs. It is possible that this has all worked out for the best, and with a bit of effort on your part, you can find new opportunities to use your true talent. Or you may have to face the fact that you have become pigeonholed. You are a long way from exercising your gifts, and to do so, you will have to reinvent yourself.

One of the most amazing examples of this was an attorney I worked with. Ryan did well enough but lacked a passion in his work. He was not aggressive when it came to getting new clients. He was bored with going to court day after day. Finally, he had to admit that he was not using his true talent. His natural gift was not expression through the spoken word in court but rather with images on a canvas. Ryan was an artist; it encompassed his intellectual property. Bravely, he left the law firm and embarked on a career as an artist. Today his paintings are hanging in prestigious art galleries.

As you unearth your true talents, you may have to go against the beliefs and expectations of others. I experienced this firsthand as a parent. My son, Sean, always had a talent for art, which he studied from childhood on. When he was 11, he wanted to take Japanese lessons so that he could read books on animation, which were written in Japanese. Despite Sean's natural talent for art and animation and a fascination with Japanese culture, I focused on another of his natural abilities. Sean was articulate from a very young age and could debate with anyone. I thought this would make him a very successful attorney.

Sean went to McGill University in preparation for law school but quickly learned that this was not his true passion. He wanted to use his creativity in animation. Today he has created his own animated cartoon, and these same characters are featured on a line of backpacks and accessories that he has designed for a prestigious luggage company. I'm proud that my son was able to recognize and embrace his true talent for artistic expression at such a critical time in life instead of launching on a career tangent that would have taken him in a totally different—and less satisfying—direction.

PERSONAL POWER VERSUS TITLE POWER

Focusing on your true talent—your intellectual property—will help you to become more discerning on the career path ahead, particularly when you are at a crossroad of choices. The decision of whether to take another job, transfer to another division, or strike out on your own will be easier to make if you first ask yourself the key question: Does this new path honor my true talent? If so, then your chances of success will be increased greatly. If not, what looks like a 24-karat opportunity may turn out to be fool's gold. Of all the glittery distractions in the business world, the one to be most wary of is the *title*.

Many people look at power from the skewed perspective of title as part of a corporate caste system. By doing this, however, they pigeonhole themselves in a system that may not always be in sync with their best interests. Marvin was an executive vice president of a large mortgage and lending institution. While he was very successful, enjoyed his job, and was very wealthy, he did not have the title chief executive officer (CEO) that he craved. After the mortgage bank merged with another company, Marvin decided to take a buyout. With more money than he needed, Marvin sailed into the sunset—literally. He went back to his native Australia and a purchased a 35-foot sailboat.

After a while, Marvin realized that he missed the corporate world. He needed to feel productive. Soon thereafter he became a highly paid consultant, providing leadership and insight to startup companies. Once again he reaped the financial rewards of his talent, but he still did not think of himself as successful without the CEO title. Finally, he got his chance at the helm of a Dallas-based firm. The problem, however, was that while he had the title he always wanted, the position did not play to his strengths. The board of directors at the firm was very "old school" and resistant to try any of Marvin's ideas to revitalize the company. The board blocked him at every turn, and he was miserable. He was not using his leadership and vision, which had made him a success in the past. All he had was the CEO title.

What Marvin learned the hard way was the difference between the appearance of power and real *personal power.* Regardless of your title—whether you are the chief executive or a first-year intern—access to your full personal power comes from the development and deployment of your intellectual property.

DIVERSIONS AND VOCATIONS

You may be lucky enough to find your true calling in the professional world. You may know that you were born to be a manager, a financial advisor, a team leader, a salesperson, a designer, or a teacher. Or you may end up in a career because of a combination of circumstance and chance, in a job that you do well enough but without passion and a sense of mission.

As you explore the concept of your intellectual property, undoubtedly you will have to sort through a number of diversions to find your vocation. A diversion is an activity that you enjoy very much but which is not a bona fide career path. While an important outlet for creativity or physical expression, this diversion cannot be the main focus of your professional endeavors. For example, you may find your solace in the garden. The physical activity of digging in the earth and the satisfaction of tending the plants may be an important part of your life. You may even wonder if you should give up your career in order to pursue landscaping. Only you can answer this question. However, diversions, hobbies, and leisure pursuits can lose their luster when they become a "job."

THE AGE OF SPECIALIZATION

Emphasizing your true talent positions you for the best opportunities while eliminating others. This process of elimination, while a natural-selection process, may be uncomfortable or even frightening for you. In an effort to be more marketable, you may have tried to be all things to all people. However, such a widespread and scattered focus leads to mediocrity and not a true specialty.

John's specialty was in the area of finance. Instead of focusing on his true talent, however, he longed to be "useful" in other positions. Thus he avoided the corporate finance jobs where he could have distinguished himself and opted to try a variety of marketing and sales positions. Meeting with only limited success, John moved from job to job. He would get dissatisfied with what he was doing, or his employer would become disillusioned with him. I worked with him twice in corporate outplacement. Both times John avoided looking at the root of his problem. He was trying to climb the corporate ladder by being all things to all people. His obvious talent for finance—a gift he underestimated because it came so easily to him—was ignored despite my best efforts to coach him. Until John recognized and valued his true talent, he was destined for a frustrating career path.

Today we are returning to an age of specialization in which we are not pigeonholed by industry—but specialists by function. In the field of medicine, specialists are sought out for their expertise. The orthopedic surgeon who operates exclusively on hands and feet has a depth of knowledge and experience that is admired and sought out by his or her colleagues. In the Middle Ages, artisans and workers would specialize in one particular area until they gained a reputation as a *master.* If you were a glassblower, you would work that craft until you were known throughout the land as a master of it. You would not dabble on the side as a woodcarver or a weaver. That belonged to the masters in those fields.

Today, whether you are a financial wizard or a creative genius, this intellectual property is the root of your past success and the promise of a brighter and more fulfilling future. Wherever you work, whatever industry you go to, this specialty must go with you.

PUTTING IT ALL TOGETHER

Uncovering, acknowledging, and marketing your intellectual property is a process. It begins with discovery and assessment and continues with strategies and implementation of action steps:

- *Assess your current situation.* What do you like most about the job or position you have now? What do you like the least? What opportunities do you have to use your expertise, and which ones would you like to have?

- *Create a vision.* If you had a job that used your intellectual property, what would it look like? What would you be doing every day? How would your expertise be showcased and recognized by others?

- *Identify roadblocks.* What is stopping you in your current position from using more of your intellectual property? Are you willing to "give away" your expertise to others? Are you speaking up enough and taking on new tasks before you are asked? Are you afraid of isolating yourself from possible opportunities by focusing exclusively on what you do best? Does your boss recognize your intellectual property?

- *Establish a strategy to overcome the roadblocks.* Commit to doing whatever it takes to use your true talent in your job. Let others know what you can do by offering to chair a committee or join a project or volunteering to help.

Now, move the timeline for your strategy out 3 to 5 years. What job would you be doing that would tap into your expertise and true talent? Can you see yourself performing those tasks and handling those responsibilities? What complementary skills and experience would you have to acquire to make this dream a reality?

Rebecca was off the fast track. For years, she had been one of her boss's favorites, and he championed her at every turn. Over the past year or so, however, Rebecca felt that she had fallen out of his favor. Her boss offered her fewer opportunities; he turned to her for input less and less. She complained bitterly about this to me. Her career path was in jeopardy because her boss was no longer willing to promote her and champion her.

What Rebecca could not see, however, was that the real obstacle to her success was not her boss's attitude but rather her own unwillingness to manage her relationship with her boss. Instead, she was allowing herself to feel like a "victim" of his change in attitude. I helped Rebecca establish a strategy of immediate and long-term goals for how she could showcase and promote her unique abilities. First, however, she would have to confront her boss.

One morning she confidently walked into his office and sat down. "Now, I know you have wanted to see me. You haven't heard from me nearly enough lately," she said, half joking and half seriously. Acting more empowered, Rebecca shifted her boss's perception of her and reestablished a stronger relationship with him.

Success is not a gift that is bestowed on you by someone else. Success is the by-product of determination and opportunity. When you are committed to your true talent—your unique intellectual property—you can give the world the best that you have to offer. You can make a difference.

Conveying Confidence and Savvy

In the business world, you are your product. Your vision, your intellectual property, your expertise, and your know-how are all part of what you bring "to market," whether as an entrepreneur, an employee, or an executive. As with any product, it is important to consider the packaging. For you, your "packaging" is the professional image that you project—the way you look, act, and appear to others. The appeal of your professional image will move others to see you as successful and, as a result, to be open to your ideas.

When dealing with the concept of image, however, it is important to state that this is not a superficial endeavor to mislead others or to foster the perception that you are something that you are not. Nor is it about looking pretty or handsome to get attention. Rather, looking confident, meticulous, and well groomed will complement the ideas, expertise, and business savvy that you possess—and that you wish to broadcast to others.

In many ways your professional image is like the cover of a book that draws people's attention. As the saying goes, however, you can't judge a book by its cover. Indeed, your professional appearance, like that book cover, helps you to be noticed in a positive light. Then it is up to the "content" to do its job. If you look good but lack substance, the appeal of the cover will fade quickly.

All too often people downplay the importance of a professional appearance. They shrug it off as "window dressing," "showing off," or somehow being "phony": *This isn't a beauty contest. It doesn't matter how I look as long as I perform and do a good job.* This kind of thinking, however, completely misses the point. Developing and projecting a successful, professional appearance is about you being your best. Like an attractive frame that enhances a painting, your appearance should help to project an appealing image about who you are, your confidence in yourself, and your own recognition of your self-worth.

The importance of a professional image has been a focal point of countless executive coaching sessions that I have given over the years. Those who have a clear appreciation for the power of visual appearance tend to grasp this concept. They are the individuals who have been marketing themselves all along in their professional circles. Those who have resisted this concept often are the ones who are left behind.

Moreover, whether we like it or not, professional appearances do matter. The moment we see another person—before any words have been spoken or greetings exchanged—we have made several observations and assumptions based on that person's physical appearance. You may have the most professionally written résumé with credentials galore, or you may be the most eloquent and convincing speaker during a telephone conversation. This may get you an appointment with a prospective client or a job interview. At your face-to-face meeting, however, unless your professional image matches what you wish to project, you will sabotage your chances for success.

Fascinating academic research has been done on the "instant impression," which validates the notion that all of us make snap judgments and decisions about others in the first few minutes—and often the first few seconds—of an encounter. A May 2002 article in the *New Yorker* took an in-depth look at first impressions.[1] According to the article, two Harvard University colleagues showed videotapes of teachers to viewers who then rated each person based on a 15-item checklist of personality traits. The length of the videotape? Ten seconds. "The observers, presented with a 10-second silent video clip, had no difficulty rating the teachers on a 15-item checklist of personality traits. In fact, when [one of the professors] cut the clips back to 5 seconds, the ratings were the same . . . When we make a snap judgment, it really is made in a snap. It's also, very clearly, a judgment; we get a feeling that we have no difficulty articulating."

In another experiment, this time at the University of Toledo, two people trained in giving effective job interviews were assigned to interview 98 volunteers of various ages and backgrounds. After the 15- to 20-minute interviews, evaluations were written out. Then an undergraduate student showed only the first *15 seconds* of these interviews to another group who had never met the applicants before. "Once more, against all expectations, the ratings were very similar to those of the interviewers," the *New Yorker* article stated.

To argue whether or not this is "good" or "justified" human behavior is to miss the point, especially since a lot of the reading of gestures, facial expressions, and outward appearances may be happening subconsciously. Rather, with the knowledge that others are going to make determinations about us based on our physical appearance, we must know how to put ourselves in the proverbial best light possible. In fact, based on what the academic research reveals, the image we project is an important determining factor in how receptive others are to us initially.

Professional image is the big picture composed of many details, which together convey the impression of who you are. These details include wardrobe, grooming, poise, body language, and voice projection. The right physical appearance substantiated by expertise equates to a winning presence.

I conducted a seminar in 1991 for a utility company that, in the midst of reorganization, was requiring employees to reinterview for their positions. Imagine the reaction from people who had been with the company for 20 years! Not only were they having to interview for their own jobs, they also were being interviewed by external people who did not know them. The incentive, however, was a powerful one. These employees were exceptionally well paid, well above engineering standards, and they wanted to hold on to their positions. Thus, whether they liked it or not, they had to learn how to market themselves.

What many of them believed, however, was that their technical expertise and their longevity in their positions should speak for themselves. They believed that their résumés said it all. The shocking message I had to deliver to them was that *within the first 4 minutes* of their interviews, the interviewer would make two important determinations: Was this employee a good fit with the new corporate culture? Did the interviewer like this person or not? All of us bring our own biases into our decision making. Thus, if the interviewers made a positive assessment, they would be more apt to be supportive of the employees they were interviewing—asking easier and nonconfrontational questions, for example, or leading them to get the answers right. This would be a big edge in the process. If the employee went on to a subsequent interview, 80 percent of the time the first interviewer sent a positive word along. If the interviewer formed a negative opinion, he or she withheld his or her support. The interviewers would be resistant to changing their opinion in the course of the interview—no matter how hard the candidate tried.

Those who capitalized on the power of the first impression were given the jobs they wanted largely because they made a conscious effort to prepare not only their résumés but also their physical presentations. This is not to say that the others were not given a job at all, but most of them had far less choice in the kinds of jobs and locations and whom they reported to.

The lesson here is that in today's competitive business environment, a holistic approach is vital to your success. It is not enough to have a good résumé, nor can you rely on who or what you know. You must put it all together, like a product you are marketing. In order for others to give your product a chance, you must have packaging that compels them to pay attention.

ELEMENTS OF A FIRST IMPRESSION

As the saying goes, you never get a second chance to make a first impression. This first impression is critical because it is the foundation on which your credibility is built. According to studies by Dr. Albert Mehrabian, professor emeritus of psychology at UCLA, when two or three people are engaged in a conversation, visual and vocal cues can either confirm or contradict what a person is saying. For example, if what someone says is out of sync with the expression on his or her face, then the listeners would put more weight on the facial expression as opposed to the spoken word. This is what is called *delivering a mixed message.* If someone says, "It's a pleasure to meet you" but has a scowl on his or her face, the listener is going to doubt the veracity of the words.

Similarly, in a phone conversation (since there is obviously no visual component), the tone of the speaker's voice takes precedence. This is called *paralanguage,* which includes the tone, pitch, and intonation that can be used to communicate attitudes or meaning. If the tone of voice is not congruent with the message being delivered, then greater attention is paid to the vocal cues. The familiar greeting "How may I help you?" may be delivered with sincerity, mechanically, or with impatience. Based on what we hear, we unconsciously put a face with the voice.

The Chinese have an interesting expression to describe a person's image. They liken it to three mirrors. The first is how you see yourself. The second is how others perceive you. And the third mirror is the truth. What's reflected in your mirrors?

Based on my work with clients, I have found that visual and vocal cues far outweigh the attention paid initially to what is being said. In sales-oriented occupations and companies, the initial importance of the visual is often given as high as an 80 percent rating. Vocal qualities (tone and pitch of voice, how confident the speaker sounds, and so forth) trail in second place, and the actual articulated message ranks a distant third. Even in occupations that are more scientific-oriented, in which you would expect a greater emphasis to be placed on ideas and concepts, the visual still is ranked the highest in importance, albeit, at a 50 or 55 percent importance compared with 80 percent in sales.

In occupations such as telemarketing, more emphasis is placed on vocal cues, which eclipses the articulated message in importance. Whether visual or vocal, these nonverbal cues hold more sway over the verbal message being received than we may have realized previously.

Several years ago I was asked to coach the sales staff at a travel company that dealt with prospective clients over the phone. To elevate their performance, I recommended a combination of visual and vocal cues to help improve their delivery and morale. While the sales team usually started the day in high spirits, by midmorning the number of rejections received from prospects often echoed in their voices. This transmitted a negative tone over the phone. This not only contradicted their positive sales script, but it also negatively affected the next call they made. The end result was a domino effect of rejection for the remaining sales calls of the day.

The solution was to put up a mirror in each person's cubicle, allowing the telemarketers to give themselves positive visual feedback. When they spoke on the phone, the sales team was told to smile at themselves in the mirror. By smiling, their tone of voice became noticeably warmer and upbeat, which made them more appealing to customers. Interestingly, the mirrors also prompted the staff to take greater care in their grooming, which made them feel better about themselves. Further, if they needed to project greater confidence in a difficult situation, they were encouraged to stand. This helped them to project their voices with greater authority. As a result of these steps, the sales calls became longer and more productive.

Projecting a strong presence is no longer an option in business. You are continually being judged by what you project.

When you showcase your physical presence, you will take greater control over the experience that others have of you. When you believe in the power of managing your impact, you will receive greater respect. (To assess your visual impact, take the quiz in Figure 4-1.) However, when you have self-doubts that nag at your thoughts and cast a pall around you, you are less likely to make an effort with your physical appearance. This could seriously undermine your career because others will make initial judgments about your professionalism and confidence based on the care you take with your appearance. The moment they see you, they will have expectations, either positive or negative. As studies have shown, when it comes to what we experience, expectation plays a huge role.

True or False

- You strategically dress for your audience.
- People notice you when you walk into a room.
- You command respect when you begin to speak.
- You leave a lasting positive impression.
- People remember when they last met you.

If you have answered all of the statements with "True," congratulations! You're on the image track for success.

Figure 4-1   Your visual impact checklist.

THE POWER OF EXPECTATION

The power of expectation was illustrated in a study in Japan on 13 people who were extremely allergic to poison ivy. Each person was rubbed on one arm with a harmless leaf, but the person was told that it was poison ivy. Each person was touched on the other arm with poison ivy and told that it was harmless. According to the *Wellness Chronicle* (December 1998) of the Creighton University School of Medicine, all 13 broke out in a rash where the harmless leaf had touched their skin. Only two people, meanwhile, reacted to the poison ivy leaves. The reason? In the field of cognitive neuropsychology, this is *expectancy theory* in action. Simply put, we experience what we perceive!

In the context of a job interview, expectancy theory is proved when your thoughts of "I'm going to mess up" or "I look awful today" undermine you. Conversely, positive self-beliefs and inner strength will enhance others' confidence in you. Whatever your thoughts are on the inside, they will shine through to the outside, thus determining the way you "package" yourself. Whether you like it or not, you are constantly showcasing how you feel about yourself with what you choose to wear. Thus, if you are tastefully dressed, you are reflecting your positive feelings about yourself.

If you are shabbily dressed or appear not to care about your appearance at all, then you are sending a negative message that tells others that you may have low self-esteem. Or you may inadvertently tell others that they are not important enough for you to dress up. In either case, what you have to say may be totally discounted. How many times has a salesperson tried to sell you clothing, but when you noticed his or her shabby appearance, you totally negated his or her advice?

Remember a time when you bought an outfit for a special occasion. Recall how great you felt when you invested in a suit that looked terrific on you. When you are well dressed, how do people respond to you? Have you noticed that you receive greater respect and attention at those times? Your appearance tells others how they should treat you.

I am reminded of a story told to me by my physician, Dr. Ron Taylor, staff physician and cofounder of the S. C. Cooper Sports Medicine Clinic at Mount Sinai Hospital in Toronto and physician for the Toronto Blue Jays. He was in an airport one day, dressed in jeans, a casual shirt, and sneakers, when he saw someone fall on the escalator. Rushing to the person's aid, he ripped his jeans, which made him look all the more unkempt. When the police arrived at the scene, Dr. Taylor was shooed away before he was given a chance to explain who he was because of the way he was dressed. "I guess I should work on my first impressions," he told me sheepishly.

FIT IN, STAND OUT

What Dr. Taylor's story shows is the irrefutable connection between what we look like and how credible we appear to others. In the business world, to project a positive, confident image, it is important to fit in with the environment that you are in. At the same time, you want to stand out. Fit in and stand out? Sounds like a contradiction. Actually, it is a subtle balancing act, one that calls for you to look like you fit in—dress in a way that is consistent with others and within the realm of others' expectations—while maintaining your own individuality. Fit your style to your desired station in life. Observe the appearance of other people whose style you admire, be it your boss, your boss's boss, your company president, or your best client. Duplicate the image that you perceive as winning. This is not to say that you cannot be original, but redefining the corporate rules of dress will only work if you first create an acceptable impression. Once you have established your credibility, then you can challenge the status quo.

When dressing for business, use your discretion at all times. Dress for your next position. Notice how successful professionals package themselves. Copy what you admire.

From the time she graduated from university, Marsha Sulewski always had a vision of where she wanted to be in her career. When she landed her first job at the Toronto Stock Exchange, however, Marsha held an entry-level administrative position. No matter, she still dressed for the management job she wanted to have, wearing beautiful and tasteful suits to work every day. In truth, she dressed in the style of her boss's boss (with the look but without the costly designer label). Moreover, Marsha carefully managed how others perceived her so that she would not be stereotyped by this entry-level job. Whenever she had tedious chores to perform, such as filing, she came in early or worked late so that no one would observe her doing this work. During the day, she was far more visible offering her assistance to others, which increased her exposure and showcased her ideas. In the end, Marsha was promoted and eventually became a senior manager in human resources. While her intelligence and her ambition got her the job, the fact that Marsha dressed and acted the part attracted positive attention.

Today Marsha is taking off time to raise her family and complete her master's degree in adult education, specializing in workplace learning and change. Her goal is to work with companies in the future as they respect the need of their staff to balance their personal and work lives. Just as she did when she was starting her professional life, Marsha is preparing to relaunch herself in the business world, both strategically and visually.

If your pride and your ego will not allow you to adapt your image to your professional surroundings, know that there may be a hefty price to pay. Often our image pigeonholes us and limits our future possibilities—without our knowing it. A case in point: Peter was a successful district manager based in Arizona. He had a very distinct renegade image, right down to his ponytail. When he would visit the small towns in his district, places that other people would not feel comfortable, everybody knew Peter and liked him. While he was very successful in his district, his image was a sharp contrast to the button-down style of the company's East Coast headquarters. Peter had his sights on a job at headquarters one day, and he probably would have cut his ponytail off to get it. But he never got the chance. Despite his success in his district, no one at headquarters thought seriously of offering Peter a job because they knew it would require him to change the fundamental way he looked and acted.

The first step to fitting in is to understand who your "market" is. Your market will vary depending, largely, on the type of business you are in. A graphic designer at an advertising agency may need to project a trendy, artistic look in order to fit in. At a bank or financial services firm, conservative dress projects credibility and reliability. Selective companies today want the assurance that whomever they hire is going to represent the company.

IMAGE IS EVERYTHING

Your professional image stamps your presence in the business world. You communicate your personality, your values, and even your willingness to be a team player and/or leader by the way you dress and conduct yourself. One of the most obvious image enigmas is Bill Gates. Enormously wealthy and yet noticeably disheveled, he has been a study in contrasts. To the outside observer, Bill Gates's outward appearance made it seem as if he did not care about how he looked or that the normal rules of the business world did not apply to him. A friend of mine was at a meeting in Chicago several years ago where countless executives, gathering to hear Bill Gates speak, actually walked right past him, not noticing the guy in the ill-fitting gray suit.

Hearing this story, I couldn't help but think that Bill Gates cultivated that image as a means to be selectively anonymous and purposefully enigmatic. Today, photos of the man worth some $40 billion (give or take a few billion) show a more polished corporate image with fashionable eyeglasses and a good haircut. Focusing on philanthropy and battling an antitrust case, Bill Gates has changed his image, as his personal packaging clearly demonstrates.

CONSISTENCY IN APPEARANCE

It is not enough to "dress up" for an interview and to look the part in the beginning. As illustrated in Figure 4-2, you must make a commitment to projecting a professional image every day. After all, you are constantly marketing yourself to others. If your appearance varies radically day to day, you run the risk of undermining your credibility.

Tammy was up for a new job and needed to "dress for success." She invested in a new wardrobe that projected the right image for her job interview, and ultimately, she was hired. Several weeks into her job, however, Tammy returned to her drab old wardrobe. The only time she "dressed up" was for senior management meetings held twice a month on Wednesdays when she made a presentation. For 9 of 10 workdays, Tammy went to work with no makeup and in her old work clothes. Every other Wednesday, she looked fabulous and impeccably dressed.

Her colleagues began wondering what was going on with this twice-a-month transformation. Did she have a job interview every other Wednesday or what? In fact, her professional image projected

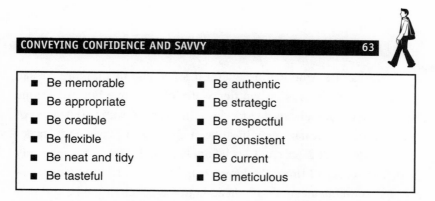

■ Be memorable	■ Be authentic
■ Be appropriate	■ Be strategic
■ Be credible	■ Be respectful
■ Be flexible	■ Be consistent
■ Be neat and tidy	■ Be current
■ Be tasteful	■ Be meticulous

Figure 4-2 The 12 "be's" of your professional appearance.

for the twice-monthly management meetings was not an asset but instead only served to draw attention to her usual disheveled appearance. The contrast was stark enough to actually raise questions as to whether Tammy had misrepresented herself in her job interview. On another level, Tammy sent a very poor message to her colleagues: It appeared she did not think they were important enough to dress up for. Only the senior management meetings were worth her effort to look her best.

LOOKING THE PART

Knowing that your appearance is a major component of your first impression, how should you dress for your next client meeting or boardroom presentation? Obviously, you want to appear meticulous, neat, and clean, with polished shoes and pressed clothes. But just how formal should you be? Should you wear a conservative suit or something more casual? The answer depends on the company and the occasion. Therefore, you must do your homework beforehand.

In the case of a job interview or client meeting, call a day or two beforehand and inquire about how people dress. Even if your inquiry gets back to the person you are meeting with, being respectful will only help to bolster your image. Keep in mind that overdressing will never sabotage your chances of getting the job, whereas underdressing carries a negative interpretation.

Corporate America in general has become much more casual. From "casual Fridays" when ties were left at home, we have gone largely to all-casual-dress work days. In the past, some 80 percent of your wardrobe dollars may have been allocated to "business corporate" attire, with 20 percent for business casual. Today it is probably the reverse. At all times, however, it is important to look and act as if you are in business and not headed to the beach or the ballpark. A few simple rules apply: The casual clothes you wear to work should be a step up from the casual clothes you wear on the weekends. Psychologically, what you wear tells others (and yourself) that you are at work and not at play.

While casual dress and "being comfortable" have long been accepted as an effective and inexpensive way to boost employee morale (at least so goes the conventional corporate wisdom), the business suit is not going the way of the doublet and tights (standard clothing in the Middle Ages). The *Wall Street Journal*, in April 2002, noted that the suit is indeed back. "Maybe it's the dot-com crash. (After all, who wants to aspire to T-shirts, jeans, and pink slips?) Maybe people are polishing their images, hoping to land a new job—or keep the current one—in a time of increasing layoffs," the article stated. "Maybe people are just sick of all-casual-all-the-time. For whatever reason, a lot of people are thinking again about suits." [2]

Caring about how you are dressed is not a sign of vanity. Rather, it is a sign of respect for others—and for yourself.

When you go to the theater, you expect the actors on stage to be dressed according to the role that they are playing. In business, while the look should reflect your authenticity, there is an element of the theatrical as well. Dress with deliberate care so that what you wear carries a message about you.

I coached Adam, a business consultant who was running a 3-day seminar at a client's office, to use his appearance strategically. At my suggestion, Adam wore a dark business suit on Monday to convey authority. On Tuesday he wore a sports jacket, tie, and dress pants to soften his image somewhat. Then on Wednesday he matched his audience, dressing in khakis and a golf shirt to purposefully encourage a more interactive, free-flowing session. Since he had already commanded their respect and earned their trust, he took the luxury of appearing as one of them.

WHAT STATEMENT ARE YOU MAKING?

People will make judgments and assumptions about you the moment they see you, sometimes consciously and very often unconsciously. The question then becomes: Do you know how people see you? If a colleague were describing you to someone who had never met you before, what would he or she say? Your professional image should be part of a well-thought-out strategy of how you want to be perceived by others.

A successful image rarely just happens. Often this is the result of careful consideration, foresight, and strategic planning.

Anyone who has ever flipped through the pages of a fashion or lifestyle magazine is familiar with the "before" and "after" pictures that depict a remarkable change in someone's appearance. These pictures are used to convey the benefit of losing weight or improving one's appearance through some means or products. While these before and after pictures are dramatic, this is not what you should be aiming for in your corporate appearance.

When it comes to your image, you must think carefully before you make even a small change in your outward appearance. After all, you are changing the packaging that you use to bring your product to market. The process begins internally with the question: What is it that you want to convey? Go back to your personal mission statement (as described in Chapter 1), and review how you want to be perceived. For example, if you want to project leadership and authority, then how does your attire project that? If your personal mission statement is to be seen as more creative yet highly competent, is this reflected in your image?

Even small adjustments or shifts in your professional appearance send an important signal to others—a signal that must be understood and heeded. You are changing their perception of you. Therefore, you must take care to ensure that the perception shift is a positive one that supports your personal mission statement.

THE FOUR CATEGORIES OF BUSINESS ATTIRE

While regional and even professional differences apply, there are generally four categories of business attire. Keep in mind that if you work for a conservative firm, you may never wear "relaxed casual" to work, whereas in a software-development firm, "relaxed casual" may be your daily wardrobe. Whatever the style, make sure that your look is consistent with that of your colleagues and those who are a step above you. You want to look like you are part of the team and present yourself as competent.

Corporate Formal

This is a suit and tie for men and a tailored suit or conservative dress for women. The suit has not lost its power, but many offices have become less formal. However, there are particular industries (particularly banking, financial services, and pharmaceuticals) in which a suit is required and many situations in which a formal manner of dressing is expected.

Corporate Casual

This is a sport coat, tie, and dress pants for men and a tailored pantsuit or coordinating jacket and skirt or pants for women. This is one step down from corporate formal and appropriate for meeting with external visitors if some formality is required.

Middle Casual

This is dress pants, cotton slacks, corduroys, or khakis; tasteful shirts (button-downs or golf shirts with collars); and sweaters for men and relaxed trousers or skirts with a blouse or sweater or casual dresses for women.

Relaxed Casual

This is relaxed slacks or jeans and a casual shirt or blouse. If jeans are permitted, a dressier version is expected. Faded, torn, tattered, and skin-tight jeans are not appropriate no matter how "relaxed" the environment.

IMAGE MAKEOVERS

Bruce was an ex-military guy with a bull-in-the-china-shop image. Gruff and demanding, he was a control freak, that is, in the business world. At home, he was far more relaxed, a trait that he felt he had to camouflage in business. His employees feared his stern demeanor, and so they steered clear of him. Employee morale was low, and turnover was high. Bruce knew that he had to change his leadership style and behavior. But he also had to change the visual perception that he was rough, tough, and unapproachable. Action and image had to work hand-in-hand.

Had Bruce suddenly begun to look and act radically different, however, the result would have been suspicion and even ridicule behind his back. Others' perceptions of you have built up over the years, for better or worse. If your appearance or behavior changes suddenly, everyone is thrown off balance. Therefore, change has to be gradual to ensure that it genuinely reflects your character. I have found that it takes a minimum of 6 months for an image shift to be completed and believed by others.

For Bruce, the first step was his glasses, a subtle signal that he was changing. At my suggestion, he abandoned the intimidating square, heavy black frames for an updated look in steel blue. People around him noticed his new eyeglass frames right away, and they even complimented him on them. While it may seem trivial on the surface, those new eyeglasses sent the message that Bruce was softening, and he even appeared friendlier. The next image change was to let his military buzz cut grow out a bit and extend his sideburns slightly, further softening his look. Bruce's actions, meanwhile, confirmed the perception that his image was projecting: He was more approachable, more willing to listen to ideas, and less gruff and domineering with his staff.

A makeover also can bring out your best features, helping to boost your confidence. Beverly was named for a top financial post, which was the pinnacle of her professional accomplishments. Her image, however, was tired and dowdy. With an updated hairstyle, makeup, and clothing, she projected a more polished and sophisticated image. It wasn't all window dressing either. In her new job she had high visibility and made media appearances and thus needed to project poise, confidence, and authority.

Just as you grow and mature, so should your image. Even in our youth-centered culture, there is value in projecting an image that is mature and confident while still attractive and dynamic. However, if you look out of date and your style never changes, you are buying yourself what I call a "permanent doctor's note" to be excused from your professional life. If your look is not current, then you are telling people that you have checked out of your surroundings. This sends a very negative message about your self-image, and you may find that your "product" date has expired.

Perhaps you think that high school was the best time of your life, so you try to preserve some physical aspect of your 17-year-old self. If this is the case, then don't be surprised if the world has passed you by. John had a beard since college, but when he was in his forties, his whiskers were gray and streaked with white. His beard made him look tired and aged and, quite frankly, behind the times. When he shaved his beard, he looked so energized and fresh that he couldn't help but attract positive attention to himself and to his business. His family, however, mocked his image change, pretending to run out of the house in horror when this "stranger" showed up.

Often, in the midst of change, you may find that your friends and your family are resistant. To them, your predictable image is part of what makes you you. Any kind of alteration has the potential to make those who are closest to you feel insecure or even threatened. Just as with your colleagues and business associates, if your family and friends see that you are acting authentically—and not putting on an act or going through a phase—they will feel comfortable with the new look and embrace it over time.

Your physical presence is like a calling card, inviting others to get to know you.

Your appearance prompts others to look for certain qualities in you and, finding them there, to experience you in a certain way. When your physical appearance supports how you would like to be perceived—whether as a leader, an innovator, a team player, or any other quality—then your audience will always be receptive to the message that you have to deliver.

Mastering the Silent Language

Imagine this familiar scene: A presenter begins a speech with the predictable words, "I'm excited to be here today before such a prestigious audience." Instead of conveying any enthusiasm, however, his or her voice is completely deadpan. The speaker's eyes are cast down to the notes on the podium, never making contact with the audience. Shoulders slump down, and hands tightly grip the sides of the podium. Excited? Certainly wouldn't seem so. Sincere? Doubtful. It would be hard to be flattered by this speaker. Although the speaker may be 100 percent sincere, the spoken words are directly contradicted by the speaker's nonverbal communication.

As this example shows, in order to demonstrate confidence and believability, you must make sure that your nonverbal communication—what I call the *silent language*—mirrors what your words are saying. The silent language consists of nonverbal signals—a handshake, a smile, eye contact (or lack thereof), a gesture, and so forth—that convey everything from the mood that you are in to your believability.

Mastering the silent language will help you to communicate your message most effectively. Moreover, it also will help you to interpret the messages of others more accurately. Whether you are the speaker or the listener, the most important elements to consider are congruity and sincerity.

Because nonverbal communication is a silent, subconscious language, you may be tempted to dismiss it. How can you push a subconscious process into your conscious mind? It is easier than you think, but it does require awareness and discipline. With practice, you will become more conscious of the messages that you are transmitting and more astute at reading the signals that others give off. Approach the silent language as you would a foreign language or sign language. The more you understand, the more in control you will feel.

Throughout my career, I have worked with countless executives, managers, and entrepreneurs on their nonverbal communication. I have seen on numerous occasions that the best ideas, the brightest minds, and the most innovative approaches can be contradicted and clouded by nonverbal communication. Typically people get so caught up in their content that they become unaware of other factors that influence their message. There is greater concentration on getting the words out than on the image they are projecting. This results in an internal disconnect between what they want to say and how they actually convey it. There is a simple antidote to this behavior: When you feel more "connected" within yourself, you take a first, important step toward bringing your verbal and nonverbal communication into harmony.

Countless tips and pointers have been written about nonverbal communication, but this is only the window dressing. The silent language becomes an artform when it is used effectively and authentically. Nonverbal communication has the power to override any attempt to mask fears or insecurities or any effort to manipulate. Put another way, words may lie, but the silent language is uncannily truthful.

SELF-CONFIDENCE AND SELF-ESTEEM

When you walk into a room with a smile and a cheerful "Good morning," you may believe that you are giving off the right image. However, if you do not really want to be there—if you are insecure, fearful, or angry; if you do not feel qualified; if you are not prepared; or if you do not trust others in that room—then your nonverbal cues are going to give you away. It could be a lack of eye contact, the distance you put between yourself and others, a fidget or nervous habit, a tense facial expression, or excessive smiling like the proverbial Cheshire cat. Why do we suddenly act defensive and challenged instead of self-assured? It ultimately comes down to self-confidence and self-esteem, which have a direct impact on our nonverbal delivery. These two highly emotional qualities are the basis of our behaviors, which reflect how we feel about ourselves.

Self-confidence is based *internally* and comes from the knowledge and security that you know your content and that you have mastered an area of expertise. You feel good about the job you are doing. Self-confidence is the by-product of good survival skills. You have been through a lot, and you have come out the other side—wiser and more experienced. Perhaps you did not do all that you could in a particular situation, but there is comfort in knowing that you are a survivor. You know that whatever you confront in life, you have the ability to cope. This self-confidence is the foundation of the "home" that you inhabit internally. You know that the "house," as depicted in Figure 5-1, can weather virtually any storm that comes along.

Self-esteem is based *externally* and can be as changeable and fleeting as the weather. Self-esteem reflects your own interpretation of how you measure yourself in relation to others. Self-esteem is also affected directly by feedback that you receive from others.

I picture self-esteem as a pie chart divided in half. The top part is looking out with optimism, an inviting refuge that beckons when you receive positive feedback. As depicted in Figure 5-2, the bottom

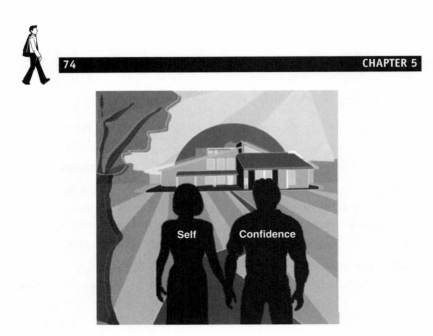

Figure 5-1   Self-confidence.

Figure 5-2   Self-esteem.

half is darkly clouded because you receive negative feedback. Your outlook is pessimistic because you believe that you have messed up or are being treated unfairly.

Sometimes you can jump from one half of that self-esteem pie chart to the other and back again depending on what you experience. For example, an important client praises your work. Your self-esteem is definitely in the "sunny half." Then additional information—or misinformation—leads to a recanting of that praise 2 hours later. Things were not as good as they first appeared. You immediately dive into the gloomy lower half. You know in your heart of hearts that you did a great job, but that perception was not shared by others. With diligence and great effort, you return yourself to the positive half.

Here's another example. Let's say that you work in the sales-support department and receive a call one day from an irate customer. By the end of the phone call, you know that you have given the best possible service. You always pride yourself on resolving issues with patience and empathy. You feel good about your ability to handle difficult customer issues, and your self-esteem is high. Then your phone rings again. This time it is your boss, who has just gotten off the phone with the customer, who accuses you of being rude and unresponsive. You can't believe your ears! As your boss demands an explanation, you feel your self-esteem sink. This becomes your vulnerability trap. When you tell your side of the story, you remind yourself that you really did do a good job, with professionalism and integrity. Fortunately, your boss comes around, but you still feel beaten up emotionally.

The problem with externally based self-esteem is that it is circumstantial and subjective and even can be influenced by office politics. Nonetheless, self-esteem always will play a role in your life because no one is ever immune to the opinions of others. Self-confidence, however, is the ideal base on which to stand. The more you build your self-confidence, truly knowing and appreciating who you are, the more you will act with strength and conviction—and the more resistant you will be to slipping into a negative mind-set. The better you feel about yourself, the more positive message you will convey through your silent language.

It's not that you should be blasé about the feedback that you receive from others. Rather, you should put it in perspective and in the context of the situation.

> **Self-esteem, based on how we believe others perceive us or how we feel we measure up, is our vulnerability. Self-confidence, based on our inner strength and knowledge that we can handle whatever life presents, is the foundation on which to build a successful future.**

TAKING A READING

We rely on the silent language far more than we realize. For example, how many times have you walked into a room and "felt" tension in the air? Most likely you have had this experience both personally and professionally. Children are very adept at reading the silent language, including when "Dad is stressed out" or "Mom's in a good mood." They know just by observing if their parents have had a fight, a sibling is in trouble, or something is "going on." Even if a child is told that "nothing is wrong," he or she will still suspect something because children are innate masters at reading the silent language.

Adults, too, can pick up on the "vibes" or "emotions" of the people in a room. This is often an instantaneous perception. Body language—facial expressions, postures, pacing the floor, and so forth—communicates how people truly feel regardless of what they say. And if someone forces a smile when they see you but you notice the tension in the person's face, it is a warning signal that all is not as it appears. I call this *taking a temperature reading,* which is registered consciously or even subconsciously the minute you interact with another person.

Have you ever walked into a room and instantly felt uncomfortable, on edge? What signals were you picking up that made you feel ill at ease? Conversely, at times when you've been well received by someone, what was it about their body language that made you feel welcome?

BE PREPARED TO BE WRONG

Each person carries around a certain amount of "baggage"—feelings, fears, insecurities, and beliefs that have nothing to do with you. You, too, have your own set of baggage. Thus, in your interactions with others, it is possible that the negativity you feel simply may be the result, unfortunately, of catching someone at the wrong time. Perhaps the person was just reamed out by the boss or received a difficult phone call. If you show up a minute later, you may feel the aftermath of that conflict. If you act defensively, however, it will be reflected in your nonverbal communication, such as anxiety written on your face. You may very well end up sabotaging your own meeting. Thus, while you take note of the "negative vibes" around this person you are meeting, keep an open mind. Instead, focus on being relaxed and showing acceptance. It is very possible that the person you are meeting in time will respond in kind to your "positive energy," and the mood will shift instantly!

It is also quite possible that what you interpret as negative may be another person's habitual behavior and have nothing to do with you. The other person simply may be oblivious to what he or she is projecting. Once again, instead of reacting with negative behaviors of your own, you must be prepared to "be wrong" and focus on your own positive communication. After all, your delivery of your message is the only thing you can control.

Here's an example from my own career. I was invited to meet with a potential client to discuss my services. With his words, he told me that he was interested in what I had to say. However, as I explained in detail, he looked distractedly up to the ceiling and glanced repeatedly at his watch. He rarely made eye contact with me, and at times his eyes were closed.

To be truthful, I was put off by his behavior. However, I recognized that I had two distinct choices. One would be to cut the meeting short; I did not need this kind of treatment, after all. The second was the realization that I had put a lot of time into preparing for the meeting and that I had value to add to his company. Therefore, I was going to give it my best shot. In response, I became more conscious of my own nonverbal cues and deliberately smiled at him and spoke with confidence and friendliness in my voice. In my mind, I imagined that he was very happy to be meeting with me. When the allotted time for our meeting ran out, I asked if we could meet again the following week. To my surprise, he agreed.

Our second meeting was at a restaurant. Over lunch, he was visibly enthused about my services and eager to hear more. He asked many open-ended questions that required me to explain in detail. It was a far different meeting than our first encounter. At the end of our lunch meeting, I broached the subject with him. "Could I be honest with you?" I asked. "I'm delighted to have the opportunity to meet with you again, but I was shocked that you agreed to a second appointment."

"Why are you so surprised?" he asked me, genuinely puzzled.

"In our first meeting," I explained, "you looked rather distracted and conscious of your time. You kept looking at your watch. I was concerned that I might be wasting your time."

"No, Roz," he explained. "I wasn't distracted at all. That's how I listen! It's funny; people say that to me all the time."

Had I merely taken his nonverbal communication at face value and reacted defensively, I would have missed a second opportunity to meet with him and ultimately work with his company.

Does that mean that you should always ignore someone's closed gestures or unpleasant facial expressions? Absolutely not. There will be other times when you will perceive correctly that someone is *not* open to what you have to say. You must be extremely diplomatic in these situations. If you are meeting with someone for the first time, be conscious of your own body language, tone of voice, and gestures. Ask open-ended questions of the other person. Be more passionate in what you have to say, and use more inflection in your voice. Observe the other person to see if he or she warms up to you. Do not act defensively, and do not be judgmental. If the person truly is not interested in meeting with you, he or she may cut the meeting short. Then you have the option of trying again at another time or moving on.

If this occurs with someone whom you know well—a colleague or a longtime client—see if your own inviting nonverbal communication can elevate the mood of the conversation. If you do not perceive a shift, inquire gently if there is a problem that the person would like to talk about. Or perhaps you have just come at a bad time, and would the person like to reschedule? At all times, however, maintain a relaxed and confident tone. If the person is truly having a "bad day," he or she will be very appreciative of your sensitivity.

We cannot focus on only the words that we hear. Reading others' nonverbal cues helps us to understand what's really going on, including how receptive they are to us. But be prepared to give someone a second chance. Leave your ego at home.

SABOTAGING YOURSELF

There are times, unfortunately, when you sabotage yourself with your nonverbal communication—when how you communicate casts doubts on the message you have to deliver.

Here's a painful little story from the early days of building my business. In those first few months I spent countless hours calling on prospective clients to develop my business. Finally, I secured an initial meeting with a prestigious prospective client. I was excited but also very apprehensive. Walking into the plush boardroom, where I was greeted by four senior executives, my discomfort was apparent. I took solace in the fact that I had done my homework and could answer any question that they asked. But how I communicated had a far greater impact than what I had to say.

After the meeting, my contact walked me to the elevator. "How do you think it went?" I asked him, anxiously. "Do you want the truth?" he asked.

My heart sank, but I wanted—and needed—to know the truth.

"They found you to be somewhat reticent. You did not come across as self-confident or comfortable. They perceived you as rather hesitant."

Thinking back, I realized that I had been intimidated by that boardroom setting, which obviously had come through loud and clear in my body language. Feeling self-conscious, I had literally shrunk into a smaller space and had spoken too quickly. I rattled on with the answers at times, not giving the others a chance to ask a follow-up question.

In the end, I was very fortunate to have received this honest feedback. Yes, fortunate. Most of the time no one will speak up and tell you how you are perceived. If you are not aware of what your nonverbal language is saying, you risk repeating situations that do not produce the desired result.

UNLOCKING THE SILENT LANGUAGE

Looking more deeply at the role of the silent language, examine your own body movements and gestures. Do you convey a confident persona, or are you still sabotaging yourself with gestures that might reflect a low self-esteem? Are you conscious of giving out mixed messages? For example, many people sit with their arms crossed, chest high. This gesture, however, can be interpreted as defensive, meaning, "Don't bother me," or even "I challenge you." For a woman, crossed arms may project submissiveness or defensiveness. In reality, she may be crossing her arms simply because she's cold! For a man, crossing his arms may be habit or a comfortable stance. It may be interpreted, however, as confrontational or aggressive. One way to safeguard against mixed messages is to seek out feedback. Ask a colleague or partner if you display any habits or body movements that undermine your message.

Does your body language convey a negative or conflicting message that you are not even aware of? What do your facial expression, posture, gestures, and tone of voice convey about you? Are they in direct conflict with who you are or how you truly feel?

I attended an owners' association meeting at a condominium complex recently at which the treasurer delivered an update to the membership. At the end, he stood for a moment, hands on his hips, intensity etched on his face. "Does anyone have a last question about the budget?" he asked. No response. He walked brusquely away from the podium and into the audience. He waited and asked for questions again. No hands were raised. No nods of agreement.

Later the treasurer told me that he took that as a good sign. Clearly, the association members had understood his message and agreed with how the budget was going to be allocated. I gently suggested a different interpretation. His body language was confrontational and not welcoming of questions or feedback, sending a far louder message than his query about questions from the audience. If he really wanted to invite a discussion, he should reconsider his body language—gesturing with his arms open and raised slightly, palms extended upward as if reaching out to the audience. Using a friendlier, less authoritative tone of voice would have been more inviting.

Leaning against the podium in a more relaxed stance would have made for a more comfortable atmosphere.

BODY POSTURING—OPEN/CLOSED, FORWARD/BACK

Body movements and gestures are very often learned behaviors that vary from culture to culture. In North America (the focus of this discussion), our multicultural society notwithstanding, we communicate "liking," as opposed to "disliking" through closer physical proximity. We stand closer to people whom we like or know very well; we tend to put more distance between ourselves and strangers.

Body postures in general fall into two categories: open or closed, forward or back. When a person uses an open body posture, arms relaxed at one's side and body turned toward another person, this indicates openness and receptivity. When a person has a closed body posture, arms crossed and angled away, this indicates that the person is rejecting someone's message. When a person leans forward toward another, it indicates liking or responsiveness. Conversely, leaning back or standing away from the other person is distancing and may project negative feelings.

Body Posture "Strategies"

- *Open/forward.* Voice your thoughts or sell your ideas when you observe someone leaning forward with steady eye contact. This posture denotes especially active listening and potential acceptance of your message.
- *Open/back.* Provide more facts and figures to corroborate your message when your listener displays an open body posture but stands or leans back. The person may be listening but may not necessarily agree with you. Practice the "pregnant pause" to give the person time to digest the information and encourage feedback.

- *Closed/back.* Be prepared to end your conversation and try again later if your listener displays a closed and back posture. This may be an indication that someone is resistant to your message. Try asking open-ended questions to encourage the person to express what he or she is thinking. Show genuine interest in the other person's point of view.

- *Closed/forward.* If your listener displays a closed and forward body posture, with head-on eye contact, tread lightly! This may indicate the other person feels some hostility. If you sense high emotion, then angle your body slightly sideways to assume a less confrontational posture. Soften your tone of voice, open your body language, and encourage the other person to talk.

PERFECTING YOUR POSTURE

Your own body posture will convey how you feel about yourself and those around you. To stand with presence, keep your back straight, assume a relaxed position, and keep your eyes and head level. Avoid stiffness, which can suggest arrogance and inflexibility. Let your arms hang loosely at your sides so that you are free to gesture. Keep your hands out of your pockets. Stand with your feet apart, parallel to your shoulders.

John was a big man, standing 6 foot, 4 inches, with an athletic build. Instead of having a commanding presence due to his physical stature, he tried to contain himself. He slouched so as not to tower over others, and he shuffled his feet as if to pass by unnoticed. The motivation behind his demeanor was his desire not to intimidate. The perception of others, however, was that he was apologetic. He tried so hard not to offend anyone that he came across as uncomfortable and lacking self-confidence. Instead of others appreciating his efforts to tone down his size and his presence, his movements were a distraction.

Working with John, I helped him to see that his physical presence was part of who he was. Denying that presence was creating conflict within himself and with others who perceived this gentle giant as someone who was ineffective. I helped him to realize that he could stand and walk tall—literally—without bullying others. Over time, he became more comfortable walking with his chin up, with a stature that was reassuring but not overpowering. Because he was acutely aware of being taller than other people, we worked on spatial distances—how close to sit or stand next to another person. For example, John would look for an opportunity to sit down if someone was noticeably shorter to avoid towering over the other person. John was self-conscious about his large hands, so he learned to make smaller gestures to the side rather than toward another person's face. Overall, he became more confident and relaxed in his stature. As he loosened up, so did others around him. For John, it was not a matter of adopting nonverbal language that was false or stiff but rather encouraging him to be more comfortable in his own body.

You may have the best of all intentions when you act or appear in a particular way. Perhaps you do not want to appear to be a show-off or intimidating. The actual impact of your behavior, however, may be the exact opposite of your intention. Asking others for feedback will help to correct mixed messages.

Posture Tips

- *Straight shoulders convey an authoritative and proud image.* This posture tells others that you have a healthy self-esteem and encourages others to notice and listen to you. Stooped shoulders convey self-dislike or insecurity. Sloped shoulders make you look submissive.

- *Stand tall.* Imagine a string attached to the top of your head, pulling you upward. When you stand tall, you tell people that you are ready to face life head-on.

- *Avoid closing yourself off by holding your arms across your chest.* An open posture demonstrates willingness to communicate.

- *Do not rock from side to side or back and forth.* Keep your weight balanced over your center of gravity. Plant your feet solidly on the ground, slightly apart, and parallel to your shoulders.

- *Direct your body physically and psychologically toward your listener to show a willingness to communicate.* Leaning too far back signals passivity and perhaps withdrawal. To encourage someone to feel more comfortable with you—particularly if you sense some unease on their part—face them directly with your head and shoulders but turn your body at about a 20-degree angle. This will give them your attention while allowing you to appear nonconfrontational.

- *When you are walking, let your arms swing naturally at your sides, forward and back.* Hands are open and your thumbs pointed slightly outward. This will give you the air of walking with purpose.

EYE CONTACT

The eyes, as the saying goes, are truly the windows to the soul. Through your eyes, you give others almost unerring insight into yourself. Making visual contact indicates that the communication channel is open. When you want to stop communication, your eye gaze diminishes. Or if you are uncomfortable or feeling embarrassed, eye contact is broken. You probably tend to make more eye contact when you are actively listening. When you are speaking, most likely you make eye contact at the end of a thought or idea, which will provide instant feedback on how you are being received. When you are warmly and favorably received, you will make better eye contact. In general, too little eye contact may demonstrate anxiety, whereas too much may be intimidating.

The Nonverbal Dictionary of Gestures, Signs, and Body Language Cues, by David B. Givens, Ph.D., of the Center for Nonverbal Studies, notes that a "highly emotional link [is] established as two people simultaneously observe each other's eyes." He adds that gazing into another person's eyes arouses "strong emotions," and as a result, "eye contact rarely lasts longer than 3 seconds before one or both viewers experience a powerful urge to glance away."

The amount of time you look at someone should depend on the purpose of your encounter, the comfort of the recipient, and the spatial distance between you. Eye contact becomes less threatening the farther away someone is.

Corinne was a medical doctor who attended one of my seminars. When she spoke to the group in practice sessions, she would look above their heads instead of making eye contact with people in the audience. The feedback from the group was that Corinne was disconnected from them. She gave the impression of being very self-focused and aloof. In fact, Corinne's lack of eye contact was the result of a technique she had been taught at college to combat nervousness when speaking in public. What she never realized, however, was that it kept her from being an effective communicator. While it was a challenge for Corinne, she made the effort to make eye contact with her audience. This calmed her down and gave her cues as she spoke. For example, an approving nod would show that her message was being received and understood.

Tips for Making Eye Contact

- *When you are in friendly conversation, you will tend to make more eye contact.* In a sales or other influencing situation, increased eye contact can make the conversation seem more congenial and casual.

- *Try smiling with your eyes.* Think a pleasant thought, and your eyes will appear warmer. This will help you to appear more relaxed and approachable.

- *To avoid looking confrontational, use the "triangular" method.* Look at the person's left eye, then the right, and finally the mouth.

- *If you are feeling uncomfortable with another person's gaze, break eye contact under the guise of taking notes.*

FACIAL EXPRESSION

Taken together, your face and eyes are the most expressive parts of your body. Facial expressions have the power to establish rapport with others. Facial expression will tell others if you are approachable, friendly, interested, confident, and alert. Conversely, a blank, stone-faced look with no eye contact says "Stay away!" An expressionless face also may suggest that you are not listening, may be bored, or are apathetic.

There are many stories about politicians, entertainers, and others in the public eye whose public persona—to their detriment—is quite different from their private or "true" natures. One case in point is Bob Dole, who in the 1996 presidential race against Bill Clinton often was perceived to be dour, which was reflected in his serious facial expression. Bob Dole, however, is famous in political circles for his dry humor, such as in his postcampaign writing, including the book, *Great Political Wit.* He also showed a surprisingly candid and human side when he appeared in television ads for Viagra.

Facial Expression and Communication

- Smiling conveys happiness and self-assurance, inspires confidence, and makes others feel good about themselves.

- A smile can confuse an adversary. Make sure that your smile is sincere, though, and does not look forced.
- Coordinate your facial expression with your words. During his presidency, Jimmy Carter often smiled inappropriately when he spoke about such serious topics as the national deficit. It negated the seriousness of the subject and damaged his credibility.
- The position of your head is also revealing. A level head projects confidence and improves posture and voice quality.
  - A bowed head suggests insecurity, submissiveness, or shyness.
  - Tilting your head to the side may suggest that you are confused or submissive.
  - Excessive nodding may make people think that you are overly anxious, too eager to please, or not really listening.

WARM OR COLD: HOW DO YOU COME ACROSS?

Another perception transmitted by your behavior is how "warm" or "cold" you are—meaning how approachable or aloof. Being aware of what is considered warm and what is interpreted as cold will provide insights into how others experience you. Do not be concerned if you have some cold behaviors. Few people are all warm; just as few people are all cold. However, it may be a real eye-opener to see what behaviors you exhibit (see Figure 5-3).

One final note on the silent language: Be mindful of nonverbal messages that can have different cultural meanings. I was delivering a presentation before an international group recently when I noticed that a man from Nigeria was consistently staring at the buttons of my blazer instead of looking at me when I spoke. At first I found it very disconcerting. Then I learned that, in his culture, to stare at a woman's face would be considered extremely insulting. What I could have interpreted as rude actually was meant as respect.

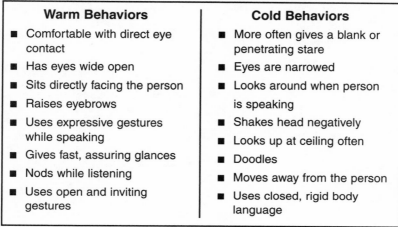

Warm Behaviors	Cold Behaviors
■ Comfortable with direct eye contact	■ More often gives a blank or penetrating stare
■ Has eyes wide open	■ Eyes are narrowed
■ Sits directly facing the person	■ Looks around when person is speaking
■ Raises eyebrows	
■ Uses expressive gestures while speaking	■ Shakes head negatively
	■ Looks up at ceiling often
■ Gives fast, assuring glances	■ Doodles
■ Nods while listening	■ Moves away from the person
■ Uses open and inviting gestures	■ Uses closed, rigid body language

Figure 5-3   Warm and cold behaviors.

As you master the silent language, you will become more articulate in conveying your message and wield greater influence in how others perceive you.

6

Building Your Professional Circle

The key to customizing your career, which ultimately will make you more resilient, is to create new opportunities. The way to tap into those opportunities is through your professional circle—colleagues, clients, and others in your industry who know who you are and appreciate your talent and expertise. Sound simple? In essence, it is a very basic, straightforward concept. What some people fail to realize, however, is that building your professional circle is not a one-time effort or an endeavor that you undertake in a panic because you have just gotten laid off. Building your professional circle lasts throughout your career.

The importance of the professional circle is demonstrated in what I call the *hidden job market*. Never advertised, never seeking applications, the hidden job market operates behind the scenes. It is the "I know someone" network that relies on reputation, relationships, and word of mouth. A professional who is plugged into the hidden job market always seems to be in demand. A boss who is tapped into the hidden job market finds the right people to hire. Without your own connection to this hidden job market, you may find yourself languishing in the backwaters of your career, waiting for opportunities that never pan out.

You already may have the exposure in business. Your name may be well known, and you may have earned a good reputation. Exposure alone, however, is not enough to preserve you in today's economy. After all, your professional circle is not just about what you do. It is about who you are and the connection that you have made with others. It is the culmination of everything you have worked on in the preceding chapters of this book: It encompasses your personal mission statement, your strategy to market your strengths and develop your talents, your intellectual property and expertise, your professional image, and your ability to connect with others through positive body language. Now it is time to put it all together and "market it" through your business network.

Building and sustaining your professional network will help you tap into opportunities that you never knew existed. And it may help you survive a potential career disaster with a minimum of bumps. Consider a recent article from the *Wall Street Journal* that stated chief knowledge officers (CKOs) and chief learning officers (CLOs) had been in demand in the late 1990s.[1] The article noted: "Then came the collapsing stock market, corporate belt-tightening and a backlash against technology, all of which prompted many companies to scrap knowledge-management posts.

"But some CKOs have survived, even thrived, by judiciously distancing themselves from the original craze, while still exploiting the concept. Their staying power demonstrates how even managers closely associated with the most ephemeral trends can reposition themselves to remain relevant," the article continued.

In other words, while their high-tech job titles were passé, professionals who remained current and strategic found themselves in demand and distinguishable from the rest. They did this by marketing who they are and their portfolio of talents, not just their connection to a title that is no longer seen as applicable to today's market.

BUILDING YOUR LIFE RAFT AHEAD OF TIME

No one wants to think about the catastrophes that might happen. And yet it pays to be prepared. One of the best ways to be ready for any eventuality is to continually develop and nurture your business network. I call this *building your life raft ahead of time.* You may need it to rescue you from the sinking ship of a company that eliminates your job in a round of layoffs or to build up your business after the demise of your biggest client. Perhaps this will never happen to you, but a life raft will come in handy to help you navigate transitional times. This support against the unknown consists of people who serve as advisors, role models, or just a shoulder to lean on. To ignore the importance of this professional life raft is to put your career in peril.

Geoffrey had been employed by a large bank for 15 years. A nine-to-five man, he was dedicated to his job, but he made it a point never to "mix business and pleasure." He never discussed his personal life at work. He had never invited colleagues or business friends to his home. There was an impenetrable wall between these two facets of his life. While he preserved a sense of privacy about his personal life, Geoffrey paid a high price.

Geoffrey's job was eliminated when the bank merged with another financial institution. As part of his outplacement package, Geoffrey was given 3 months to create or find another job within the new company. At the end of 3 months, if he did not have another position, he would have to leave. Networking at the company for the first time, Geoffrey found it difficult to connect with others. Given his standoffish behavior for the previous 15 years, others were less than eager to go out of their way to help him.

Working with executives in outplacement over the years, I have seen and heard so many situations like Geoffrey's. Based on this experience, I also can say that the length of time an executive uses out-placement services is absolutely determined by the network that he or she has built over the years. Those who enter and exit outplacement rapidly usually are the ones who not only have expertise—there are a lot of experts in the business world—but who also have developed a professional circle over time. When they need it, there are plenty of people who are willing to champion them, recommend them, or even hire them.

If you think your professional network is a one-way street designed only to benefit you, then you are sorely mistaken. Your professional network is a circle—with no beginning and no end. The help that you give to someone today will come back to you when you need assistance or support. It is truly a case of "what goes around comes around." This is not to suggest that you give only to get. Rather, your professional network is reciprocal arrangement whereby everyone benefits.

In his book, *The Seven Spiritual Laws of Success,* Deepak Chopra describes the "law of giving" as benefiting both the one who gives and the one who receives: "If you want joy, give joy to others; if you want love, learn to love; if you want attention and appreciation, learn to give attention and appreciation; if you want material influence, help others to become materially affluent. In fact, the easiest way to get what you want is to help others get what they want."

THE IMPORTANCE OF RAPPORT

If you have not yet built a professional circle, you may be wondering how to accomplish this. It begins with your interpersonal skills—your ability to connect and communicate with other people. Using these tools, you build rapport, which is the foundation of any relationship. When you have rapport with others, amazing things can happen. A whole new world of relationships and opportunities will be open to you.

Through rapport, even the most seemingly dissimilar people can find common ground, whether it is intellectual curiosity or a sense of humor—although it may require a little research on your part. Rapport leads to understanding and acceptance, which, in turn, leads to sustaining relationships and loyalty.

Of all the elements that go into a relationship, rapport is the most vital. Rapport allows another person to come into your world and invites you to experience someone else's. Without rapport, all that remains are points of views and judgments of what is "right" or "wrong."

Most people look to create rapport when they have an instant connection with someone else. They tend not to pursue rapport with someone who is dissimilar, whether due to age, culture, or background. This mind-set, however, limits your opportunities. The rapport challenge, therefore, begins with the recognition that not everyone has the ability to break down barriers quickly. Most people, to a greater or lesser extent, live in a safety zone. When you are in your safety zone, you look first at people who are most like you. Think of your friends or others with whom you had an instant rapport. Chances are that there were obvious similarities that enabled you to connect. Venturing outside your personal zone, however, you can develop a rapport with a wider variety of people and, in the process, expand your network. The process can be painstakingly slow, but like an investment, it grows over time. The more you exercise your networking abilities, the easier and more natural this process will become.

You do not have to be a brain surgeon or have a doctorate to impress people. All it takes is an outward focus and the commitment to get to know other people. This is an innate ability that we all have. If you have any doubts, think back to when you were in first grade and virtually everybody was the "new kid." As a child, you undoubt-edly had the ability to make connections and friendships easily. You haven't lost that ability. The rapport that enabled you to establish your friendships is also what sustains them.

Self-knowledge is important, but it cannot replace a con-nection with other people. People who win know who they are, have a positive and cheerful demeanor, and connect easily with others.

THE RAPPORT CHALLENGE

Building rapport begins with your own mind-set. Adopt an attitude of curiosity. Be open and genuinely interested in others. I see this as an attitude of lifelong learning: There is always something to learn from someone else. You also must be nonjudgmental. Most people like to be "right." However, when you meet someone who is very dif-ferent from you, you cannot view him or her through the judgment of being "wrong." Let the differences you observe lead you to greater understanding.

Do not limit your rapport to only a select group of people. If you develop a connection with colleagues but do not have rapport out-side your department, you may shortchange your career. If you con-nect only with the customers you serve and not with your colleagues, you may find there is no goodwill at "home" where you may need it the most.

Brian's external customers loved him. He valued them, and they knew it. But Brian had minimal connection with the people he worked with, including his direct reports. Other than the day-to-day duties of the job, he did not invest in getting to know them on a more personal level. He could communicate with them—letting his staff know what needed to be done or imparting other information—but he never developed a relationship with them.

What Brian failed to see was the very obvious benefit of developing rapport with others. He saw nothing in common with his colleagues and direct reports—other than working for the same company—and so did not invest in getting to know them. When Brian needed to rally the support of his colleagues and direct reports, however, he had nothing to fall back on. It was like trying to make a withdrawal from the bank without ever putting in a deposit.

BEING "CONNECTED"

You may like to think of yourself as being in charge of your own destiny. This, however, is not always the case. You, like everyone else in business, are influenced by other people. You, in turn, influence a host of others. Ignoring this symbiotic web in the business world can seriously undermine your career. Far too many careers have derailed because people did not connect with the right people. The decision makers simply were not aware of who they were and what they had to offer. They did not have the support of their colleagues, who were also a potential source of career leads.

I see this so often in my outplacement seminars for top executives. I often walk into a room of 15 to 20 *completely silent* people. There is no conversation, no introductions. It is as if they are each in a bubble. They fail to recognize that the people sitting next to them are potential industry contacts. My first assignment to them is immediate: "You've got 15 minutes! Talk to the person next to you. Find out who you know in the industry that this person could speak to." We then spend the next 10 minutes discussing why they acted so isolated in the first place.

It is not enough to network to find your next job. You might be able to scramble and pull enough strings to get what you need or want this time. But what about next time or the time after that? To advance your career requires an ongoing investment of your time and effort.

Roberto went to work for a company that was launching a new retail chain in Los Angeles. A real worker, he knew how to produce sales results. These numbers quickly got the attention of the senior vice president and the president of the chain. Unfortunately, Roberto did not develop rapport with executives on the level just above him. Moreover, he did not develop a relationship with colleagues in other parts of the company, such as warehouse managers and corporate buyers. He was forced to fight to get anything he needed, especially current merchandise and replenishment of hot-selling items.

In the end, when Roberto was offered another position in the company, he was not offered his dream promotion of managing the company's flagship store. Rather, given his hard work and diligence—his store had produced very strong sales, after all—he was assigned to a poorly performing store in an undesirable mall location. Disheartened, Roberto quit.

Luckily, this is not the end of the story for Roberto. He had developed rapport over the years with executives at another leading retail chain. In fact, he was more visible to them than he was within his own company. When they learned that Roberto had left his store-management position, he was quickly offered another job. However, he took with him an important lesson: He couldn't just be seen as a hero outside his company. In his new position he would need to make connections and nurture relationships internally in order to make things happen.

BECOMING MORE VISIBLE

Building rapport will improve your visibility within your company and in your professional circle. Visibility is even more important today than in the past, given the fact that corporations have become highly team-focused. The sales team, the marketing team, the engineering team, the product-development team—people are viewed in groups that work collectively toward a common goal. As a result, individual efforts may not be recognized initially. You certainly do not want to come out and say, "I did all that! I am responsible for the team's work!" This is not in the corporate value system today. The only way to get credit for your role on a team is to improve your team's visibility and position yourself as a leader. Then you will become more closely associated with the success of the project.

Leadership is not something that you demand. It must be earned. The first step is building rapport with others, which enables others to recognize your talent, your expertise, and above all, your integrity. This will make them want to follow your lead.

Improving your visibility starts with your boss. While you may assume that your boss knows what you are doing, this may not be the case. Keep your boss up to date with a monthly e-mail regarding the projects you are working on, the tasks you have completed, and even ideas and suggestions. Do not worry if your boss ultimately takes credit for the success of the team project. In the corporate world, one of the unwritten rules of success is making your boss look good. To do this, you have to be willing to share or even give up the credit.

When your efforts reflect well on your boss, everybody benefits. If you do not particularly like or trust your boss, this becomes more difficult. Overall, it is hard to increase your visibility without working with your boss. If you try to jump too many levels to increase your exposure, it may work against you. Others may perceive that you do not respect the system or that you are not a team player. Take time to nurture your relationship with your boss. When was the last time that you invited him or her to lunch? Or are you stuck in entitlement attitude, expecting your boss to take the initiative? No matter how talented you are, you cannot do it alone. Do not make your boss your enemy; make your boss your ally.

Eileen works in a company department that deals frequently with the government. She knows all the important decision makers, and she is very comfortable talking with them. Even though Eileen has been with the company for more years than her boss, this does not negate the fact that he outranks her. He holds a higher position in the company than she does. At a recent dinner meeting, however, Eileen ignored the protocol that comes with the corporate pecking order. Instead, she sat next to the top government official at the table, edging out her boss. This did not reflect well on Eileen. By side-stepping the corporate hierarchy, Eileen showed a lack of respect for the system and alienated her boss.

Improving your visibility is a lot like playing chess. You develop a strategy and make your moves, always working toward the goal of attracting positive attention to the job you do, the skills you possess, and your ability to connect with others. Don't be the "Lone Ranger" who believes that he or she does not need anyone.

Increasing your visibility strategically can earn you a higher profile within the company or business arena in which you operate. It also will help to prevent you from getting pigeonholed in a job. Often it is not some failure or lack of skill that traps you in a particular job; rather, it is because you are so good at doing a specific set of tasks or functions. Therefore, your boss and perhaps even your colleagues do not want to lose the security of having you in that position. The detriment to you, however, is that over time you may be perceived as having limited skills. Create a relationship in which your boss is completely committed to your growth.

All too often people miss opportunities to bond with others outside their own limited circle. For example, many technical people tend to stay within their own team and do not show up for corporate functions. They fail to see these social occasions as a chance to connect with others in the company. In addition, when they go to a meeting, they see themselves as gathering information. They are not there to socialize.

Another example is the new employee who immediately puts up a fence around himself or herself. Such employees are so focused on proving themselves first that they fail to establish important relationships and connections within the company. Others may get caught up in the "my department" syndrome and never venture out of their tight-knit corporate communities. And there are others who believe in keeping a distance between the business and personal aspects of their lives and in so doing isolate themselves from nearly everyone.

George was a manager at a large insurance company. A diligent worker, he put in long hours, often coming in at 7:30 in the morning and staying until 8:30 at night. He preferred to work alone, however, often with his door shut. If his staff needed him or wanted to ask him a question, they knocked on his door. George never made it his business to spend much time outside his office.

In time, George was given an opportunity to manage a new project, heading up a team of 10 people. The problem was that nobody liked George. They considered him aloof and standoffish; some even thought he considered himself to be superior. George's team did not want to work for him and therefore put forth only a minimal effort. Reprimanded by his boss for his lack of people skills, George quickly went on the defensive. He was not about to start engaging in small talk. "Don't expect me to discuss my wife and family with other people," he snapped. "My personal life is no one's business."

Unfortunately for George, he completely undervalued the human element at work. He expected everyone around him to share his laser focus on the task at hand. George couldn't manage a team, and in the end, his career suffered.

Increasing your visibility to showcase your interests and talents will require you to expand your professional circle. Social events sponsored by your company are an excellent way to get to know people from a number of different departments. Become a member of the company softball team. Volunteer for the party-planning committee.

Get involved with a corporate charity event. If there is a new initiative at the company, find out how you can contribute.

If these endeavors seem intimidating at first or require too much of a time commitment, there are smaller ways in which you can widen your circle. Speak to people in the hallways. Go to lunch with colleagues or acquaintances from other departments. Seek opportunities to ask for advice. Spend time visiting another department to see how it is run. Ask questions, and show that you are interested.

When you go to work, do not leave your social graces at home. Saying "Hello" and "Good morning," having a pleasant demeanor, and engaging in light small talk are important skills—regardless of your profession or career level. Even if this kind of "schmoozing" is not what you are used to, remember it is as important as any skill set in an office or business environment.

When you go to a meeting, do not begin with your own agenda the minute you sit down. Certainly be prepared with a list of topics that you want to address, but do not try to talk over the chitchat that precedes many meetings. When you arrive at the meeting, if your colleagues are discussing someone's new baby, you had better listen politely and seem interested. If you try to cut them off, you will not be heralded as being ultraprofessional. Rather, they will think unkindly of you.

As simple as this may sound, many people are resistant to the idea of being more social at work: "Why do I have to be conversational all the time with people at work? I spend enough time with them from nine to five. Why do I need to associate with them outside of business hours?" This may be true. However, you do spend a considerable amount of time with colleagues, managers, clients, and business associates. While they may not be your best friends or closest confidants, the fact that you share a business environment ought to be reason enough to build a better rapport with them. And you never know! The person you are snubbing today may be the decision maker on your next project tomorrow.

One common faux pas—and the biggest lost opportunity—occurs when a large group is gathered for a meeting or a presentation. As soon as there is a break, what happens? Everybody gets on their cell phones, checks their e-mail, or becomes otherwise absorbed in their own little worlds. Rarely do people look around the room at the others who are in attendance—people with whom they have an instant connection because they are at the same event—and strike up a conversation. The chance for rapport is lost, and the opportunity to connect is never pursued.

Typically, sales representatives understand the importance of people skills because their business is based on relationships. They may have the best product in the world, but unless it is the only one of its kind, they will have competition. Just look at the technology sector. Virtually any product that was unique yesterday has an imitator today and a competitor with improved features tomorrow. The highest-performing sales reps have figured out that customer loyalty is always built with rapport and nurturing relationships. (Figure 6-1 shows how you might build and expand your professional circle.)

Keep an up-to-date database of your contacts (name, e-mail address, phone number, etc.). Know what's going on with them (i.e., new jobs or promotions). Remember their birthdays. E-mail them articles that relate to their special interests. Send them personal, handwritten notes on occasion. A handwritten note conveys how important someone is far more than a dashed off e-mail. In other words, invest the time and effort to develop these contacts into relationships—and friendships. At all times, use your discretion. Not every contact will want to develop a friendship with you. And remember, your network is as much about you helping someone else as it is about someone helping you.

- AT WORK: Become part of a cross-functional team. Join ad hoc committees or other groups. Pitch-in and help others who can benefit from your epxertise. Investigate a networking program. Align yourself with high-profile individuals who can help promote you and increase your visibility.

- IN INDUSTRY: Join industry associations. Take advantage of these networking opportunities. Become fluent in the current issues. Develop a reputation as an expert.

- SOCIALLY: Become active in social clubs. Join a health club. Take an enrichment course (e.g., wine tasting). Volunteer with a charitable organization. Become involved with a school or community group. You never know where your next contact will come from.

Figure 6-1   Networking tips.

INTROVERTS AND EXTROVERTS

Making connections is easier for some people than others. Often extroverts find it easy to talk about themselves and let their opinions be known. Introverts usually are more comfortable in the background or observing at meetings instead of speaking up. Neither extreme is the ideal. Regardless of your personality type, be prepared for meetings, especially with senior managers. This is your chance to establish a connection with others who may not know much more about you than your name. Go into each meeting armed with what you want to say, ideas to offer, and observations to share.

- For an introvert, preparing ahead of time will give you more confidence. Even if someone else makes the comment that you wanted to make, voice your agreement. Let people see you as an active participant. The sooner you speak up at a meeting, the greater your visibility becomes.

- For an extrovert, learn how to draw out input from others. Be judicious about your own comments. Know when to step back and assume a lower profile. Channel your energetic and outgoing nature in a purposeful way. This will prevent anyone from seeing you as talking just for the sake of talking.

Use meetings as an opportunity to showcase others on your team. You can champion others who are not in attendance or who are not as visible at the meeting. Using phrases such as *our team* or giving credit to several individuals by name will not dilute your impact. On the contrary, it will emphasize your contribution as part of the team and demonstrate your leadership.

LISTENING: THE FORGOTTEN COMMUNICATION SKILL

Listening is a vitally important, but often ignored, communication skill. As Stephen Covey says, "Most people listen not with the intent to understand, but with the intent to reply." It is easy to be so focused on what you want to say that you do not take time to understand where others are coming from or what they really want to know. In order to listen, you must concentrate on the other person—this means looking at him or her and paying attention to what he or she has to say. This does not mean tapping your feet, doodling, making notes, or fiddling with your Palm Pilot.

When you listen to another person, you are actually giving something to that person, whether you define it as your attention or your energy. As a listener, you must adopt an attitude of empathy. Chances are that the person will respond in kind when it is your turn to speak.

There is an essential difference between *hearing* and *listening*. When you listen, you are genuinely interested in what the other person has to say, their viewpoints and problems, and what is most important to them. When you only hear someone, you are merely waiting for the pause so that you can say what's on your mind.

Tips on Effective Listening

1. Face the person who is speaking. Turn your body toward him or her. Lean forward slightly.

2. Adopt a relaxed, open posture and a warm facial expression.

3. Encourage the person to keep speaking with verbal cues such as, "Tell me more. This is interesting."

4. Subtle, occasional nodding encourages the other person to continue speaking.

5. Rephrase or summarize what was just said. Refer back to something the person said earlier in the conversation. Acknowledge how the person feels.

6. Resist the temptation to jump in. The person may only be taking a breath and may not be finished speaking.

7. When the person has finished, encourage the conversation to continue with open-ended questions such as, "What was your experience?" "Why do you believe this to be the case?" and so on.

Giles was being interviewed for a vice president position. He came to the meeting prepared to explain in detail his expertise and what he could do for the company. The president, however, wanted to take a much easier line of questioning. Giles worked for a food company, and the president was curious what it was like working there. Her family business, after all, was wholesale grocery. (Giles did not know this because he hadn't done his research. This fact was included in the president's bio on the company Web site.)

"Do you enjoy working in the food business?" the company president asked.

Giles gave a quick answer, but wanting to impress her, he launched into a monologue about cost-containment programs that he had been instrumental in implementing. He had his own agenda about what he wanted to talk about. Needless to say, Giles never got the job.

Had he really listened, Giles would have had a far different outcome from that job interview and potentially a far different career path today.

Test your ability to establish rapport with others using Figure 6-2.

THE INTERPERSONAL-SKILL INFIRMARY

As much as you try to put your best foot forward, sometimes you end up putting your foot in your mouth. Or the spotlight of recognition that you have been seeking suddenly turns into an accusatory glare. Whether you have been falsely accused or rightfully bear the blame for something, you must learn to handle these situations with dignity and integrity. Granted, this can be very difficult, particularly if you feel that you have been wronged. Here are some strategies, however, to help you keep your cool in heated situations.

---

1. Do you help people to feel comfortable?
   a. Do you take the lead? Or, do you wait for others to take the first step?

2. Do you let your personality out?
   a. Do you have a sense of humor? Do you look for opportunities to use humor tastefully?
   b. Are you approachable? Do you let people get to know you?

3. Do you need to be the center of attention, or do you share the stage?
   a. Are you a good listener?
   b. Are you genuine?

4. Are you savvy enough to discuss topics other than work and family?
   a. Can you converse in a way that makes others want to join in?
   b. Do you solicit and listen to others' opinions, or do you lecture?

5. Are you concise, or are you long winded?
   a. Do you assume that people need to hear you and everything you have to say?
   b. Do you ask open-ended questions that will further the conversation? Or, do you tend to ask closed ended questions that can *only* be answered with a "yes" or a "no?"

Figure 6-2 Rapport quiz.

When the pressure is on, appearing and acting calm will boost your confidence and be a positive influence on others. This is the essence of *grace under fire.*

False Accusations

When you are wrongly accused, it is only natural to become defensive. As soon as you do, however, you put up a potentially insurmountable barrier between you and the other person. And if you fire back with your own accusations, it may lead to an all-out war.

The first step is to identify the source of the accusations. For example, if your boss has called you on the carpet or a colleague has lashed out at you, then you know the source of the conflict. However, if you have been accused behind the scenes, meaning the rumor mill is churning with negative information about you, then you must do what you can to find out where the conflict started. It is possible that you have been set up by someone, which will complicate matters. However, by talking with others, you may soon discover the source of the problem.

The second step is to open a dialogue with the person who has accused you. Admittedly, many people would rather avoid bringing up difficult issues than to address them straight on. But what you do not address can come back to haunt you later on.

Establishing a dialogue cannot be done in anger. In fact, it may be best to wait a day until you have a chance to cool off. Then approach the other person with the clearly and calmly stated intention of resolving the issue. Let the person know what you want to discuss and why. For example, "I really need to talk to you about what happened yesterday. I want to understand how this occurred so that we can put this behind us." Or, "I want to try to resolve this conflict between us. I want to make sure there are no misunderstandings between us in the future. Please understand that our relationship is important to me."

Ask the person to explain his or her viewpoint. As you listen, try to respond rather than react. Paraphrasing what is said—such as, "I hear that you felt I discredited you when I spoke up at the meeting"—will show that you understand the other person's point of view. At no time, however, should you take the blame for a false accusation. Further, do not apologize for what you did not do, although you may express regret or concern over the conflict.

Once you have talked it out, try to reach a resolution for the future, such as being more open and candid with each other. If the conflict was with your boss and efforts to talk the problem out have not resolved the issue, see if you can hire a coach for guidance. Demonstrate your willingness to address any behaviors or communication patterns that might be misperceived or misconstrued.

If you cannot resolve the conflict, then you have two choices. If you believe that the incident will blow over without taking a hefty toll on your credibility or career path, then you can let time run its course. If you feel that the unresolved conflict is more serious and potentially career damaging, then you may want to seek the advice of human resources or a trusted advisor at the company. Otherwise, you have no other choice than to begin looking for another job.

When you have been falsely accused, you must assess if your credibility has been damaged to the extent that it prevents you from moving up or moving ahead. If so, then you must move on.

Confronting Others

A colleague has stolen your ideas and presented them at a staff meeting, taking all the credit. Rather than pursuing a head-on collision with the other person, use diplomacy to regain your ownership. In a meeting, you can "thank" the person for presenting the ideas and then elaborate on them yourself. Or engage the other person in a conversation outside the meeting.

When confronting another person verbally, you must take care not to become emotional or excessively loud. Doing so will only force others to be aggressive or defensive in return. The key is to state your case in a nonthreatening but assertive fashion. Refer to the facts and not what you assume to be someone's motive. For example, "The idea you presented at the meeting was the one I discussed with you last week." Stating the facts will be far more productive in the longer run than an accusation such as, "Why do you always take my ideas and make it appear as if you came up with them?" Avoid using *always* and *never,* which are trigger words that are most likely to cause a fight.

If the other person responds with an outburst, allow him or her to finish speaking before you respond. Avoid the red-flag phrases such as "You should . . . ," "You're wrong," or "That's stupid." When treading on emotional ground, use first-person phrases such as "I can see that we view things differently" or "I strongly disagree because . . . ," or "I would like to settle this as soon as possible." Do not bring any other grievances or complaints into the discussion other than the issue at hand. Do not mirror negative behaviors back to the other person. While this is going to require a lot of self-control on your part, the only winning strategy is to be assertive yet tactful.

Accepting Responsibility

When recovering from mistakes, misjudgments, or similar failures on your part, the first step is to accept responsibility. "I'm sorry. How can I fix this?" is a simple but powerful apology. If you have failed to do something that you promised to do, then make it right as soon as possible. If you inadvertently insulted someone, then let that person know that it was never your intention to make him or her feel uncomfortable. Try to work out a game plan so that the incident will not be repeated. While these can be difficult and awkward conversations, sincerity and empathy win the day.

If the person is too angry when you approach him or her the first time, wait to talk about it a second time. If the person still can't discuss it with you, send him or her a personalized note with your apology. Take an honest and humble tone: "I know that I have paid a big price for this mistake, and I thank you for accepting my apology."

There are times when you may accept responsibility for something that was not specifically your fault. You may decide to do this because you inadvertently offended someone or to be a peacemaker. Here's a story from my own experience:

I was presenting a seminar at a large consumer products company. I had divided the room into two teams composed of equal numbers of men and women. After I began the program, a woman came in late and sat down at a table. I asked her if she would mind sitting at the other table because I had divided the room into two equal teams. She resisted, saying that she wanted to stay where she was in order to sit with her friend. When I persisted, the woman retorted that she was only in the program because her boss forced her into it. Begrudgingly, she moved to the other table and sulked.

At the next break, I called the woman aside. "It was not my intention to make you uncomfortable by having you sit at this table," I told her. "I know you want to sit with your friend. After the break we're going to do an exercise, so I'll have the two of you sit together."

Having been heard, the woman opened up to me. Her real problem, she confided, was that her boss did not understand or appreciate her. She felt beaten up and abused. When I asked her to move away from her friend, it was the proverbial last straw. Once she was seated with her friend, the woman felt she had an ally at her side. She was a wonderful, positive participant in the rest of the program.

I had a more recent experience of acknowledging other people's feelings in an emotionally charged situation. I had traveled to another state to give a 1-day program for a new corporate client just as the war against Iraq had begun. Many of the attendees also had traveled and were obviously anxious about being away from their families— and even a little angry about being there. I did not want people's feelings about the war per se to become the only topic of the conference. But I had to let them know that I understood their point of view. Thus I began my remarks: "I know that you all have a lot on your minds these days. I, too, am looking forward to being home and safe. But for the time that I have with you today, I am committed to being totally in the present with you."

By saying what was on everyone's mind, I established an instant rapport with that group, and they responded in kind. We made the most of that day, and in the process we had fun.

The common thread in each of these difficult, emotionally charged situations is to focus on your own words and actions. By taking control of your own part, you remove yourself from being seen as the victim. You empower yourself even when you are in a position of having to apologize or accept blame for something that has gone wrong.

Taking charge of what you do is the essence of another key behavior—acting like a *host*. In the business world and in your personal life, your decision to act as a host or to remain a guest will greatly determine not only your experience but also the outcome of your interaction with others.

HOST BEHAVIOR VERSUS GUEST BEHAVIOR

There are two types of people in life: hosts and guests. First, let me define what I mean by hosts and guests.

- A *host* is an empowered person who makes others feel welcome, comfortable, and important. A host can anticipate how others expect to be treated. Hosts know that no one wants to feel embarrassed or uncomfortable or to be made to feel wrong.

- A *guest* enters a situation with a certain set of expectations. A guest wants to be made comfortable and to be heard, understood and appreciated. Guests want to be treated as if they are special. If they do not receive the guest treatment that they expect, they are instantly disappointed.

In the business arena, it is far better to be a host than a guest. Now, if you have been steeped in the "me first" society—in which you expect to be listened to, heeded, waited on, and given an upgrade to first class—then your back is probably up right now. But let me ask you: How effective has guest behavior been for you? Do you recognize how it can actually work against you?

Here's an example: You have got a great idea at work, and you really want to see it implemented. At the next staff meeting you present your idea enthusiastically, but it does not receive the reaction that you expected. Some people ask you tough questions; others just throw cold water on it. Your anger rises, and your responses become more and more defensive. After the meeting, you are frustrated and very angry. You mutter things about office politics and ignorant people who would not know a good idea if it bit them on the hand. Why do you even bother to contribute to this place?

This is guest behavior at its worst. By entering a meeting with the expectations of a guest—I will be listened to, paid attention to, and appreciated—you become bitterly disappointed when things do not go according to your plan. Your disappointment creates an entitlement attitude, which is a definite career limiter.

What would have happened, then, if you had adopted host behavior in that meeting? Let's imagine the scene: With host behavior, you seek to create a nonthreatening environment that encourages others to respond to your ideas—whether you are running the meeting or not. You ask questions with sincerity, respect, and genuine interest.

If you still need convincing, please allow me to remind you of the new stakes in the corporate game. There is no such thing as job security, regardless of your title or your years of experience. There is no such thing as entitlement. No one is going to give you a raise or a promotion because you have been there so long or do what's expected. These beliefs are woefully out of date.

In this brave new corporate world, the skillful hosts will do far better than the expectant guests. Being a host is not about being a doormat. On the contrary! As a host, you are empowered. You are not looking for others to give you something. Instead, you are contributing to a productive, harmonious atmosphere. Adopting a host mindset, you are making your own opportunities. You are committed to being successful and helping those around you succeed.

A host is a great listener, nonjudgmental, and exceedingly attentive. A host instinctively feels out the environment and understands the needs of others. They do not come into a situation expecting to be served; rather, they look for opportunities to be giving.

Adopting host behavior does not mean that you are the social butterfly of the office. Rather, it is a way of thinking and acting that demonstrates that other people matter. This will automatically make you appear warmer and more inviting. People will want to stop and talk with you. Host behavior enables you to adopt a positive, winning attitude. Acting as a host does not mean that you take over someone else's meeting. Rather, it puts you in a position of making a positive contribution in any gathering or event. You take more initiative as an active participant.

I had an experience recently that really crystallized my thinking on host behavior. I needed a second surgery to correct an injury to my Achilles tendon, which wasn't healing properly. I was in the Canadian health care system, which has a reputation for scarce resources. Knowing what could happen, I prepared a host behavior strategy.

What I really wanted was a private room, something that is not always available in Canada. When I got to the admitting desk, I put on a big smile and asked for the "honeymoon suite." This comment got a laugh, broke the ice, and landed me in a private room. On the eleventh floor, I chatted with the nurses about a very interesting book that I was reading. I promised to share my insights with them if I was able to get not only a private room but a corner one with a view. Done!

Settled into my room, I made a sign on the back of a paper plate that read, "The Honeymoon Suite—Please Visit," and taped it to my door. Curious staff and other patients stopped by. My hospital room soon became the hospitality suite, which interestingly allowed nurses and staff to network with others whom they did not normally see on their shifts.

When the nurse asked me to change into a faded, drab blue robe, I issued a mock complaint that I look deathly ill in that color. "Couldn't I have one of those bright yellow robes like some of the other patients?" I asked. The yellow robes were only for isolation patients, she explained. But when I promised to hide in my room and not tell anybody, I didn't have to wear the ugly blue one.

Here's the point. Through host behavior, I was able to make the hospital staff laugh and feel appreciated, and they reciprocated. I understood from the beginning that hospitals are severely short-staffed and that the nurses are overworked, underpaid, and rarely complimented. With no expectations of the system, which I knew could be very frustrating, I created my own positive experience through host behavior.

Are You a Guest or a Host?

- Do you think small talk is a waste of time?
- Do you avoid after-hours meetings and social events?

- Do you often leave meetings feeling frustrated and misunderstood?
- Do you prefer working with your office door closed?
- Do you protect your time from meetings and incoming calls?
- Do you answer unnecessary telephone calls while you are in a meeting in your office?
- Do keep your cell phone on and your Palm Pilot out when you meet with others?
- Do you show up late for meetings with your colleagues but arrive on time for senior management meetings?

If you answered "yes" to five or more of these questions, you are displaying a tendency toward guest behavior. Nonetheless, you can experiment with host behavior. You will be surprised at the positive reaction that you will get and how you will feel as a result.

As a host, you will naturally champion people, and they will respond. Even years later, they probably will remember you and the respect that you show to others.

Michelle was on the fast track at an advertising agency. In her late twenties and pregnant with her first child, she was promoted to vice president. After a brief maternity leave, she was back at work. Years later, when she was pregnant with her second child, her perspective changed. She wanted to take off 6 months. Her boss, however, became angry with her for not coming back to work sooner. He demoted her and reduced her salary. Disappointed, Michelle reached the conclusion that she had to leave.

She started her own firm with one employee. Within a few years, several staff members from her former employer's company had come to work for her. The rapport that she had built with her former colleagues was so strong that they wanted to work for her—even when they had to take a pay cut as she grew the business.

The reason for Michelle's success—beyond her incredible talent and business savvy—is that she is a natural host. She always championed those around her and refused to be dragged down by an unappreciative boss. Clients who heard through the grapevine that Michelle had started her own company sought her out. Her own good fortune greatly benefited many people, and today her business is thriving.

A final word on host behavior: Never underestimate the importance of the small things. A compliment, a thank-you note, a gesture of goodwill. Nothing is ever wasted.

Making Presentations—Connecting with Your Audience

You are asked to make a presentation at an upcoming event. Regardless of whether it is a 15-minute talk to a small group of your peers or a 45-minute speech to an industry gathering of hundreds, your reaction may very well be the same—dread. The fear of public speaking is common to many people, including those who make presentations on a regular basis. To counter this apprehension, people often focus on their content. They know what they want to say and how they want their PowerPoints to look. They think that if everything can be perfect, then they will do just fine.

And this, unfortunately, is a recipe for failure.

The *perfectionist syndrome,* as I call it, is a trap. You can become so caught up with everything being right that you put too much focus on yourself and your content. Then, when one small thing does go wrong, you and your presentation can easily unravel.

The bigger problem with the perfectionist syndrome, however, is that it puts the main emphasis in the wrong place. Contrary to what you might believe, making a presentation is not about what you know. It is not about how much you have to say and the dazzling visuals that you can produce. Rather, it is all about the audience.

To be a successful presenter, you must first understand the expectations of others. Why are they coming to the presentation, and what are they hoping to learn from you? Being able to answer these questions is as important for a 3-minute talk given at a staff meeting as it is for a 45-minute speech before an audience of hundreds. Operating from this perspective, you can turn your natural fear and apprehension into powerful tools that help you to rise to the occasion and give your best presentation ever.

Most people have fears and apprehension about speaking in public. Those who are masters of communication, however, have learned to override their superficial fears about looking good. They know they have important information to share, which the audience wants to hear. Their value system is geared toward making a difference.

Presentation skills are vital to anyone's career, even if you never give a formal speech. Most people are asked, from time to time, to give a report in a meeting. Mastering presentation skills will help you to convey information and explain details easily and succinctly. However, I do not believe that presentation skills end there. In fact, I will go so far as to say that you make a "presentation" each time you come in contact with another person. In your day-to-day interactions, you are constantly presenting ideas, facts, and opinions to others and responding to their "presentations" with comments and questions. Whether you are engaged in a dialogue or are speaking to a group of 5 or 500, there is one underlying rule that always applies: Know your audience.

WHO'S YOUR AUDIENCE?

Identifying your audience (as depicted in Figure 7-1) is the first step to putting together a successful presentation. If you are speaking to a group of colleagues at an internal meeting, you already have a head start in this process. If you are speaking at an industry gathering, the composition of that audience is less certain. And if you are asked to be a guest speaker to another industry, conduct research to understand your audience's needs, points of view, and values.

Jeff Ansell, who is skilled in leadership communication, believes that the key to a successful presentation is to focus on the delivery of one thought at a time. "Instead of doing a 'download' or a 'mind dump,' a speaker must gauge the audience's response to each thought that is delivered," explains Jeff, who is an associate in the Public Disputes Department at Harvard Law School and my partner in our 2-day "Art of Wow" leadership conferences.

"Don't focus on whether the audience agrees with you. Rather, are they confused? Is there something that you said that you need to build on? Too many people, when they give a presentation, focus on themselves. When that happens, however, they fail to make that vital connection with the audience," Jeff adds.

---

1. Identify who will be in attendance.
2. Define your relationship with them.
3. Determine what you have in common with them.
4. Assess how knowledgeable the audience is in your area of expertise.
5. Evaluate their level of interest in the topic.
6. Pinpoint potential areas of conflict.
7. Consider any special circumstances that could impact your presentation.

Figure 7-1   Who is your audience?

THE COMMONALITY CONNECTION

As you identify your audience, one of the key components is to consider the commonality connection. At the opening of your presentation, you must be able to establish instant rapport with your listeners. Through your experience, your background, or even your point of view, you must demonstrate that you understand where each person in the audience is coming from. If you are perceived as coming from "a different place," know that you will have to take deliberate steps to show that you understand your audience.

Here's an example from my own career. As a communications and image specialist, I have a strong grasp of my content. In other words, I know that my expertise and the information I bring will benefit my audience. However, unless the audience believes that I understand them, they will be resistant to my message. Thus my job as a presenter is to understand their day-to-day world.

Since I present to so many different industry groups, I have gone to great lengths at times to comprehend more fully the daily business needs of my clientele. I have spent the day with cable television installers, riding in the truck and going house to house with them to deal with customers. I can recall being dressed in overalls and steel-toed boots talking to a customer with full-body tattoos who was wearing nothing but his underwear with a snarling Doberman at his side. After a day of going up poles and climbing into attics, I had a deep appreciation of and respect for what cable installers had to go through every day.

I have also gone out with the Labbatt's beer trucks, visiting customers from small neighborhood stores to large retailers and restaurants. At the end of the day I understood what it was like to sell in such a diverse marketplace. The bottom line is that as a presenter, you must convey that you have "walked in the shoes" of your audience (sometimes literally!) in order to establish a sense of commonality up front.

SHORT PRESENTATIONS

Knowing your audience and making the commonality connection are also important when you give a short presentation to an informal gathering, such as at a staff meeting. While you may not consider your 2-minute report to update your colleagues on a team project to be a full-fledged presentation, let me assure you that it is. While the written word is powerful, it cannot compete with the spoken word presented live to an audience. When others see you and hear your voice, there is an emotional connection. Even if the spoken word is delivered one-way—from you as the speaker to others listening to you—it is part of a dialogue. Others respond, if not verbally, then with nonverbal communication that tells you everything from whether they understand you to whether they agree with and support you.

A true leader understands the power of the presentation to communicate directly with others. Never has there been a leader who led others only through e-mail.

THE STAFF MEETING

Your boss comes to you with a request to make a 2- to 3-minute presentation about an ongoing project at the next team meeting. This is an opportunity for you to showcase yourself and to be seen, at least for the moment, in a position of leadership. In many ways these informal presentations have more impact than a formal speech because you can really focus on the listeners and read their body language more clearly. But you still must prepare for this presentation, just as you would for a formal speech.

- *Do your homework.* Since you have been asked to give the update, you obviously know something about the topic. Nonetheless, you should seek feedback from others who are involved in the project ahead of time. What are their main issues and concerns? The more you involve other people as you prepare your talk, the more support you will have when you give it. Let your boss know ahead of time—in person, not by e-mail—what you will be talking about. This is not a time for dropping any bombshells or springing any surprises.

- *Know the audience.* What information does your audience want from you? If everyone in the meeting has been involved with the project from the beginning, there is no need to provide in-depth background information. Rather, what your audience probably wants is information about the project status, deadlines, delays, and next steps.

- *Highlight the key points.* Keep your presentation to one or two main points. Start with those points, provide details, and reiterate them at the close. Practice your presentation until you are comfortable delivering the material.

- *Focus on delivering a polished but relaxed presentation.* If you can, get to the room where the meeting will be held ahead of time to choose your seat. If you are gathering around a conference table, take a seat in the middle so that when you stand to speak, you will be able to address the entire room. Even if you have only a short time frame, slow down. There is no need to rush to say everything in only a few minutes. Speak in a relaxed, conversational tone, but make sure to project your voice enough so that everyone can hear you.

- *Make eye contact with every person in the room.* Begin and end with the person you are addressing. It is critical that you look at those people with whom you want to actively engage in a dialogue. This will ensure that they do not become preoccupied with their own thoughts and miss your point entirely, particularly if you want them to support your ideas. As you speak, move your eyes slowly from person to person, pausing briefly to look at each face. Do not neglect those who are on your immediate left and right, even if you have to turn to see them. This will help you to maximize your visual presence when you speak.

Even if you only speak for a minute or two, you can make a lasting impact with a focused, succinct, and informative presentation. For example, I worked with a group of professionals from various company divisions who gave 10-minute presentations twice a year to the president of the corporate holding company and other senior executives. What they said in those 10 minutes made the biggest impact on how they were viewed by senior management for the rest of the year.

Invest in your personal impact. The more you make short, informal presentations, the more natural it will be for you, and the more comfortable you will become with public speaking. This may open opportunities for you later on. You may be called on to address a larger meeting, company conference, or even an industry gathering. When these opportunities arise, remember that the only real differences between a formal speech and a brief presentation are the length of the time speaking and the size of the audience. All the other key points of making presentations, which we will review in this chapter, apply. The two most important rules, however, are (1) know your audience and what they expect to learn from you and (2) know your subject matter.

CONTEXT VERSUS CONTENT

Keeping the audience's perspective in mind will help you to define the *context* of your speech. Context always takes precedence over *content,* which is what you have to say and how you want the audience to apply it. Context, however, answers the question, Why is this important to my audience? Answering the "why" question upfront before you give information provides your audience with the motivation to listen to you. Have you ever heard a speaker who never captured your full attention? Was it because the speaker failed to give a reason to listen?

Does your audience want more information about a particular subject? Are they looking to hear both sides of an argument to help form an opinion? Are they learning about a new product or technology? Do they need information to make their businesses more productive? What are they seeking to lighten their workloads, increase their success, or improve how they do their jobs? Once you determine the context, the content will flow.

Every person listening to you wants to know, "What's in this for me?" Your presentation must clearly and succinctly answer this question.

Starting with the context also increases your emotional connection with your audience. Ironically, putting the audience first also will act in your best interest. Even if you make a mistake or your nervousness comes across in your tone of voice, your audience will be more forgiving because you have put the emphasis on them—and not yourself. If the intention of your speech is to appear impressive or to elevate your standing, then the focus will be on you. People will form an opinion about you, not what you have to say, and the result may not be favorable.

I remember the first seminar I conducted. I was so nervous that I literally heard my knees knocking. I did not face the audience enough. I kept turning my back to the audience to read my slides. From a presentation perspective, this is a major faux pas. However, I really believed in the value of my message. I cared about my audience, and they felt it. The end result was that despite my less than polished speaking skills in those days, the audience connected with me and with what I had to say to them. I have learned that given the choice, audiences prefer to listen to someone who is authentic but not polished rather than self-focused individuals who are on a mission to impress.

Do not think that your title and your credentials are going to be enough to get a buy-in from the audience. Speak from your heart. When you make an emotional connection with your audience, they will listen to you and believe the message that you deliver.

FACT AND EMOTION

Many people, as they begin to write their speeches and develop their PowerPoint slides, dive immediately into the facts and figures. Indeed, logic plays a very important part in reaching your audience on the conscious level. Straightforward facts—that is, a new product led to a 20 percent increase in sales for the company—will help you convey your message. But logic and information can't tell the whole story. In order to reach your audience and hold their attention long after the presentation is over, you also must communicate emotionally. This subconscious connection relies on your listeners' intuition to ascertain if a message is true for them. When they connect on an emotional level, the audience will be more apt to absorb the factual, logical information that you present (see Figure 7-2).

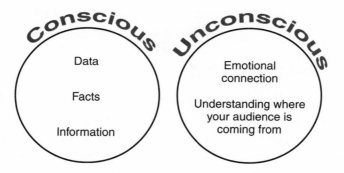

Figure 7-2 Conscious and unconscious connections with your audience.

A medical supply company developed an innovative piece of equipment that could sterilize medical instruments in a fraction of the normal time. This breakthrough represented a major cost savings to hospitals. The problem, however, was that soon after the product was launched, glitches were discovered. The equipment did not perform consistently.

The research team that had been assembled to produce this equipment had gone on to new projects at the company. Now they were being reconvened. When the vice president of the medical supply company addressed them, he knew that his message was not merely a financial one—the impact on company sales. Nor was it just about the performance of a product. In order to get the team recommitted to the product, he had to reach them on an emotional level.

He opened his speech with a slide showing his 3-year-old son joyfully eating an ice cream cone. "When our customers receive our new sterilization equipment, this is how they feel," the president said.

Then he switched to the next slide of a fierce electrical storm. "This is how our customers feel when they realize that the integrity of our equipment is not to be trusted."

Every person in that room recommitted to that project not just on a professional level—but on an emotional one as well. As a result, the problem of the equipment was resolved very quickly.

As this example demonstrates, it is important to identify what values your audience holds. Addressing those values in your speech will facilitate an emotional connection with your audience.

FOCUS ON A SINGLE MESSAGE

Too often presenters try to tackle too many points in one speech. They have so much to say that they try to cram it all in. As a result, however, the audience may feel bombarded instead of informed. In presentations, the "less is more" philosophy applies. First, determine your main theme, and make sure that everything you say relates in some way to this major point. For example, if your speech is about customer loyalty, you are not going to address new product development.

Think of your main theme as the hub of a bicycle wheel. The points that you make—whether through facts, personal anecdotes, or case studies—are like the spokes that radiate from that hub. The spokes provide structure to the wheel, but at all times they are connected to that hub. In the same way, everything you say to develop, illustrate, and convey your points must relate back to the hub or main idea of your presentation.

As you prepare for your speech, your greatest efforts should be placed on your opening. Too often people focus on the content and let their opening remarks take care of themselves. As long as they have the facts and figures, they tell themselves, they can ad lib the opening. What they fail to appreciate, however, is that the opening "hook" is the most important part of their speech.

Your opening is the most important part of your speech. Once you have the opening, the rest of your content should flow automatically. Memorize the first few sentences so that you will be able to look at the audience from the beginning.

You might choose to open with a story that illustrates your main point. Make it a personal anecdote, which will help others to view you as one of them. Avoid opening with a joke. Most of the time, jokes fall flat, and sometimes they even turn off (or offend) the audience.

Whatever the actual content of your opening remarks, the purpose should be to establish a connection with the audience. Even if you know that some attendees outrank you or have more industry experience, you must project a self-assured demeanor. Never be so self-deprecating that you tell your audience that they know more than you do.

One technique that I have used is to include a kind of testimonial in my opening remarks. "You may have had different experiences than I have. My goal today is to share my personal perspective with you. Many of my clients have told me that the strategies that I am going to discuss have been useful in their professional lives." Or you may decide to acknowledge the different skill sets, levels of experience, or needs of the audience by saying something like this: "Some of the information I have to share may be of use to you immediately, whereas other parts may be prove to be valuable in the future."

WHAT YOU SAY, HOW YOU SAY IT

Knowing what you want to say, the next step is to determine how you can best say it. Content and delivery go hand in hand; the two are inseparable. Basically, there are two ways in which to deliver a speech: *tell mode* and *share mode.*

Tell mode is a one-way lecture. You are demanding that your audience listen to you instead of inviting them to participate in the discussion. Your underlying message will be that you have all the answers and that they had better pay attention. Most people, however, do not like to be told what to do, and they may react negatively. Make the assumption that 20 percent of your audience will be skeptical initially. Your audience may tune you out or even become confrontational with antagonistic questions and comments. When you are *telling,* you may appear to be self-focused, and it may seem that you do not care about their opinions and perspectives.

A far better approach is to share—information, research findings, personal experiences, expertise, and so forth. When you share, you are inviting your audience to participate. You engage your audience intellectually and personally. You acknowledge that they, too, have opinions but that you have something to contribute to the discussion as well. Even though you have information to present, when you are in share mode, you increase your ability to be persuasive.

One way to reinforce share mode is by using the word *you.* Often companies use *we* and *us* to engender the feeling of being part of a team. However, when you use the word *you,* your comments are automatically personalized. It is as if you are speaking to each member of the audience individually. For example, after introducing a point or making an observation, I encourage people to personalize the information with a few simple but subtle questions. "Do you often feel that way?" I'll ask them, looking around the room. "Have you had this experience?" Or I will put it in the form of a statement or directive. "Think back to a time when you experienced . . . ." Careful and intentional use of the word *you* will help put your listeners in the right frame of mind.

THE POWER OF THREE

As you organize your speech, keep in mind the *power of three.* Being able to summarize or condense your topic into three points will help your audience remember while keeping you, the speaker, on track. I read a fascinating article on the power of three in the Toronto *Globe and Mail* by communications skills coach James Gray.[1] "The number three has astonishing power in communications—we organize, explain and retain information more efficiently when it's arranged in 'threes,' even from an early age," Gray wrote.

In the article, Gray illustrated this point using the example of a media interview. "For example, . . . you could say: 'Our programs are valuable to the people for three reasons—one, they create employment; two, they help the environment; and three, they save taxpayers money."

I can tell you from personal experience that the power of three also works in presentations. When I want to emphasize key points, I condense them down to three ideas. Standing before the audience, I state them one by one, counting on my fingers. Summarizing in three points holds your audience's attention and increases retention. Using your fingers to count each point deters the audience from interrupting you.

Strive to summarize throughout your speech, emphasizing the key points that you want to deliver. This is especially helpful after you have presented a new argument or additional data.

KEEPING TIME

Being able to summarize the key points of your speech will serve another important purpose. Even if you are scheduled to give a 45-minute presentation, you should be able to deliver the key points in far less time. Let's assume, for example, that because of a scheduling problem, your 45-minute program has been reduced to 20 minutes. Or perhaps the speaker who preceded you greatly exceeded his or her time. What should you do? Cram everything you have to say and every slide you have prepared into 20 minutes? Should you insist on speaking for the full 45 minutes, even if you end up disrupting the rest of the schedule?

No matter how complex your topic, you should be able to condense it into a far shorter time frame. Admittedly, you will have to eliminate some of the details and skip many of your slides. However, if you cannot deliver a shorter version of your speech succinctly and yet in an engaging manner, then you have put too much into your program in the first place.

The Gettysburg Address, one of the greatest speeches every given, was less than 300 words in length. When Abraham Lincoln delivered it, his audience was spellbound. Initially, he mistook their silence for rejection of his message. However, as the story goes, a member of his audience remarked that applauding Lincoln's speech would have been like applauding the Lord's Prayer.

Now, I ask you, if Lincoln had spoken for 45 minutes, would he have made a greater impact?

Speak for less than your allotted time. Your audience will appreciate it if you do. If you start to run long, they will start paying more attention to their watches than to you. Being conscious of your audience's time is a sign of respect to them. It is not that you want to shortchange them, speaking for only 5 minutes instead of 30, but if you speak for, say, 25 minutes instead of 30, then you are telling others that their time and attention are valuable.

As a speaker, never look at your watch. Rather, use a small clock with large numbers on the podium, hidden from the audience's view.

No matter how long your presentation, keep in mind that your listeners have a limited attention span of somewhere between 15 and 20 minutes. In his book, *The Articulate Executive,* Granville M. Toogood talks about the "18-minute wall," after which the audience will rapidly lose interest.[2] His advice is to keep any presentation to 18 minutes and then to open up for questions and discussion.

While that may not always be possible, you must still heed this rule. One option is to break your speech up after 18 minutes or so. Think of a scene shift in a three-act play. With a small group, you might want to engage them in an exercise, preferably one with some type of physical activity. For a larger group, you can lead them through a mental exercise ("Close your eyes and envision . . ."). Or you may shift gears dramatically from a presentation of facts into a personal story. Use your own movements to reawaken the audience's attention.

USING VISUALS

Slides, overheads, and other visual aids help to highlight key points and enable the audience to grasp certain concepts. The problem, however, is when visuals are used to excess. They are not meant to be read to the audience, like subtitles in a foreign-language movie. Rather, the audience, at the prompting of the speaker, should refer to the slides. Graphics that illustrate a point are far more effective than endless lines of small, hard-to-read text.

I remember being at a convention at which several members of a company were going to speak. The vice president of human resources and three national sales managers spent hours rehearsing and rerehearsing their speeches. They had numerous slides that illustrated every possible point. The human resources executive had nearly 100 slides! The president of the company also addressed the group. In command of both the context of the speech (what the audience wanted to know) and the content to be delivered, he had six slides. As you can imagine, the president had far more impact on the audience than the executives with their overkill presentations.

While visuals can enhance and illustrate your presentation, do not rely on them to convey your message. In fact, you should be prepared to make your presentation without overheads or slides. This will help you to deliver your message effectively in the worst-case scenario should the projector go on the blink or your slides suddenly come up missing. Do not use slides as a substitute for your own ability to keep track of the flow of your material.

> **Never use audiovisual equipment that you can't fix. Keep in mind Murphy's law—if something can go wrong, it will. This law seems to apply especially to audiovisual equipment used for speeches. Do not assume that someone in the audience will perform a lifesaving operation on the equipment!**

Another means to introduce visuals into your presentation is with *word pictures*. A description that conjures up an image in your listener's mind is far more powerful than anything you can create with PowerPoint. Word pictures rely on the images that are common to all of us to visualize the message, i.e., the stormy seas of turbulent times or smooth sailing with the wind at your back.

Anticipate. Anticipate. Anticipate. Think about what issues you might face. Consider the problems that you could encounter. Know what your audience's reaction will be. At all times, focus on how important your message is to the audience. This emotional connection and your passion about the topic will carry the day.

FACING FEARS

As you prepare for your presentation, anxiety may confront you at any time. If you feel apprehension, take heart! You are in good company. Even experienced presenters have stage fright now and again. The best antidote to the jitters is to turn that anxiety into energy. Recognize your fear as nature's way of preparing you for any eventuality. Let it heighten your awareness and sharpen your mind. This positive use of fear also will counteract your "internal saboteur." If you allow negative thoughts—"I am going to mess up; I am going to embarrass myself"—get the best of you, chances are that you will end up with a self-fulfilling prophecy of disaster.

Also keep in mind that you have far more empathy from others than you may realize. Everyone realizes that it can be difficult to speak in public, and most people have the same fear. Thus, when you get up to speak, your audience is pulling for you. They do not want you to fail. The more passion you have for your message, the more you believe in what you have to say, the more committed you are to the audience, the more you will be able to overcome your fear. And even if you do make a mistake, the goodwill you have established with your audience will help you to get back on track.

You may be fearful because you know that your topic is contentious. There may be strong opinions in the audience, and you could face stiff opposition to what you are saying. If this is the case, then bring that conflict right out into the open at the start: "I know that there are strong opinions on this topic, and that the debate is far from over. My purpose today is to examine some of the issues and to provide you with some insights that may help you to make an informed judgment."

I had been hired by the managing partner of a law firm to present a 2-day program to attorneys to polish their presentation and communication skills. The attorneys were being forced to go out and market their services to new clients through half-hour presentations. The attorneys resented these sessions, which they called "beauty contests." Making matters worse, often they would run into lawyers from competing firms while waiting in the lobby for a turn to make a presentation to the client. When the firm announced my program—which would look at everything from the way the attorneys dressed to their interpersonal skills—it was not warmly received. Some people at the firm took to calling it "charm school."

The morning of my program, the managing partner called me aside and warned me about the resistance to the program. I told him not to worry. I knew how to diffuse this kind of situation.

"Rumor has it that some of you think of this as charm school," I told them right at the start. I could read the look of surprise on many of their faces.

"Well, let there be no mistake. This is not charm school— although I can be quite charming." I paused as they laughed lightly.

"The purpose of this program is to improve your ability to market yourselves and your firm to prospective clients to ensure your professional future and the longevity of your firm."

That was the last I heard about "charm school."

I brought home to those attorneys that day the "new reality" of the business world. Your expertise, your ability to connect with and communicate with others, your presentation skills, and your appearance are all part of the total package that you use to market yourself. If you are lacking in any of these areas, you will undermine your chance for success. Worse yet, if you offend someone by what you say, if you act or appear in any way inappropriate, you will suffer a loss of credibility that will be difficult, if not impossible, to overcome.

As a final note on preparation, while it is important to have strong command of your content, never memorize the entire text (with the exception of the few lines of the opening). If you do, your speech may sound overly rehearsed and insincere. Practice speaking from notes so that you sound more natural.

ON THE BIG DAY

After days, weeks, or even months of preparation, the day has finally arrived. Now it is an hour or two before "show time." Where should you be? In your hotel room or in some quiet corner practicing your speech for the 4000th time? No! Your place is at the event. If another speech precedes yours, then you must "scope out" the venue well in advance. This means studying the layout of the room, taking note of where the exits are, how the seating is arranged, and so forth.

If I can, I soundproof the doors of the room where I will be speaking. Using heavy electrical or duct tape, I cover the latch on the door. In this way, when someone enters or leaves the room during my speech, the audience will not hear the door open and close.

If possible, walk on the stage where you will be speaking. Be familiar with the placement of the stairs up to the stage. Will you have easy access to walk out into the audience if you need to? Test out the microphones. Stand in the lights and determine if you can still see the audience. If there is a podium, will you be able to walk around it? I like to turn the podium on a 45-degree angle to the audience. This allows me to use the podium without it blocking their view of me. Another tip for podium placement: Position it so that you will be at the audience's far left and the screen is at the far right. Since in this culture we read from left to right, make sure that the audience focuses first on you and then moves to their right to view your slides or overheads.

As the speaker, do not be shy about asking for things to be adjusted for your comfort and the success of the program.

A podium for a speaker is like a double-edged sword. On one hand, it is part security blanket and part note holder. On the other, it is a barrier that can separate you from your audience.

In addition to checking out the venue for your speech, you must connect with your audience in advance. This means working the crowd. If another speech precedes yours, show up at the coffee break to chat with people outside the presentation room. If people are coming into an auditorium or meeting room to hear you, position yourself inside the door. Talk to them as they seat themselves. Greet them and thank them for coming.

Whenever possible, I walk the aisles before a speech, shaking hands with members of the audience. Sometimes I tell them who I am, and on other occasions, I remain anonymous—hoping to hear some candid feedback as to why they are there. The better the connection I can make before a speech, the greater my chances for a successful presentation that meets the needs and expectations of my audience. The reason is that when we meet people and establish a positive connection with them, we lay the groundwork for empathy. As a speaker, when I address a crowd after I have made "friends" in the audience, I know that I am beginning with people on my side. They are pulling for me. They want to me succeed, which shows in their attentiveness, the nonverbal cues they give me (nodding and making eye contact), and their level of participation.

While I am working the crowd, I may arrange in advance for volunteers that I can call on during my speech. When I call on Susan or John in the middle of my presentation, it affirms the impression that I am speaking as one of them and not as an outsider.

The more successful you are working the audience before a presentation, the greater are your chances of engaging your listeners.

HOSTING AT THE PODIUM

When you speak, you must adopt *host behavior.* As discussed in Chapter 6, when you act as a host, you are in control. You anticipate the needs of others, and you encourage discussion and dialogue. Nowhere is host behavior more important than when you are speaking in public. If you are on the defensive, if you have expectations about what the audience will do for you, then you are in *guest behavior,* which will undermine both your impact and your credibility.

As a host, you must be mindful that when you are addressing an audience—whether it is 10 people or 1000—you are engaged in a dialogue. While you may be doing most of the talking, the audience is also communicating. A nod, a gesture, eye contact, laughter, and even the occasional murmur of agreement (or disagreement) is part of the dialogue.

Involve your audience as much as possible. If the group is small, you can lead a discussion or ask for feedback and comments at different points throughout the presentation. Or, in a larger group, encourage them to take notes. Interject a few simple phrases: "Write this down. It's an important point for you to remember." The audience will automatically focus on what you are saying. The act of writing something down also will help them to remember your message.

Do not try to impress your audience with your vocabulary or your vast technical knowledge. As a host, you strive to keep your speech simple and to the point. This will enable you to hold your audience's attention and gain their respect.

As a host, you take it on yourself to connect with every person in that audience. One way to do this is with eye contact. In a small group, say, of 25 people or less, it is fairly easy to look at each person in the room. If you are nervous, it helps to focus on a friendly, smiling face. However, do not become glued to one person to the exclusion of everyone else. Let your eyes slowly and calmly look from person to person, focusing a few seconds on each. Remember, the greater the distance between you and someone else, the longer your eye contact can last. If someone is close to you, then eye contact that lasts too long can seem confrontational or may make the other person feel uncomfortable.

The larger the gathering, the more difficult eye contact becomes. In an auditorium setting, you may be blinded by the lights, making it impossible to see your audience, other than the people in the front row. Nonetheless, you must give the audience the "feeling" of your eye contact. To accomplish this, my friend and colleague Jeff Ansell uses what he calls the *baseball technique.*

Here's how Jeff explains it. Instead of "playing tennis"—with your eyes going back and forth rapidly—he suggests "playing baseball." This means that when you focus in the audience, you envision hitting a ball to someone. Your eyes focus on that person for the length of time it would take for the ball to be caught and thrown back to you.

When shifting your focus on a large audience, I use the concept of an hourglass (see Figure 7-3). Starting at the center, you trace an hourglass shape with your eyes slowly over the audience—from center to far right, across the back, to the far left, center, near left, across the front, and near right. Repeat this process several times during your presentation to ensure that your focus doesn't become glued in one spot or on one group of people.

GESTURES

When you speak naturally, you probably use your hands. These gestures help you to emphasize a point or show animation, interest, and

Figure 7-3 The hourglass technique.

even emotion. The same holds true when you make a presentation, with a few adaptations. The larger the audience, the bigger the hand movements should be. Avoid the "Velcro syndrome," with your hands stuck to your sides. Using broad, sweeping, and open gestures will help embrace and capture the interest of a crowd. Make sure, however, that your gestures are smooth. Broken, rapid, and jerky hand and arm movements are a distraction and actually can make your audience feel unsettled.

Use your gestures in conjunction with your words. This is especially important when addressing a larger group. If you raise your arms and open your hands as you say, "I am delighted to be here today to address this distinguished audience," make sure that your gesture lasts as long as your words. If your drop your hands at midsentence, you will lose the impact. When you gesture, make sure that it is from waist level upward. This helps keep up the energy of your presentation. Gesturing downward is a negative cue that lowers your energy. (If you want to watch some masters at gestures, watch television evangelists who know how to hold a crowd's attention.)

Some people like to stand with their hands behind their back. If so, then use "parade rest," with your hands in the small of your back and elbows out at the sides. This will naturally make you stand straighter with your shoulders square. However, make sure that you don't appear to be handcuffed and that you are able to gesture in a relaxed and confident manner.

Learn the art of the pause. This can be used for dramatic effect or strategically to help you shift from one topic to another. And when it comes to the unplanned pause—you lose your place or forget the point you were about to make—remember that it is never as long as you perceive. The hesitation that seems to last an eternity probably does not last any longer than a few seconds. Do not be afraid to pause because of the false perception of a time gap. Another good use of a pause is when you are asked a question. Pausing a few seconds will allow you to arrange your thoughts succinctly and avoid being long-winded. If you give yourself permission to pause, it will eliminate excessive "umm-ing." One final note on the pause: Look down momentarily, which will make you appear more introspective. Looking up makes you appear to be searching for answer.

CROWD CONTROL

When you make a presentation, be prepared for the critical comment, the antagonist who drones on and on, or someone who is disruptive. If a member of the audience makes an opposing comment, try to find some point of agreement—no matter how small. If you cannot agree, then try to find some common ground, such as the comment, "Clearly, this is an important issue that needs to be addressed." When you are asked a question, take a step closer to the person who is speaking, even in a large audience. Then step back when you reply in order to involve the whole audience in what you have to say. This also can help you to prevent one person from monopolizing your attention.

Do not answer too quickly, and do not look away hastily, because that can be interpreted as cutting the other person off. An effective strategy to curb someone from dominating the discussion is to firmly but diplomatically intervene. "It's not fair that you and I do all the talking. How about someone else in the audience asking a question? Don't make us do all the work." Another way to diffuse a potentially volatile conversation is to offer to speak to the person after the presentation.

If someone is visibly upset or antagonistic, you must take charge of the situation without being aggressive or defensive. Do not let yourself become angry or lose control, even if you feel under attack.

I was making a presentation to company executives on the psychology of boardroom seating when one of the executives interrupted me with an outburst. "This is a lot of hocus-pocus," he said, throwing his day-timer on the floor.

For a moment, I wondered what I should do. Then I quickly recalled my host behavior. This man obviously had a problem, which I, as the host, had to address in a positive and yet disarming manner. I walked over and stood close to him. I couldn't show that I was annoyed with or intimidated by him. I looked at him with great compassion and concern and said, "I can see you have a lot of passion around that statement."

By stating the obvious, I cut through his negative emotion. "What I believe you're asking for is the validity of what I'm saying." By rephrasing his confrontational question, I gave myself the dignity of being able to answer it. Even though he may have deserved to be put in his place, I would have lost face if I had belittled him. My goal was to not alienate him and to keep the audience on my side. After restating his question in neutral language, I then proceeded to explain the research that backed up what I had been saying.

MESSING UP AND MUDDLING THROUGH

The only way to truly become a master presenter is by dealing with just about any mishap, mistake, mess, or mix-up that you can imagine. If you make an error, do not apologize. Just correct yourself if you have misspoken and keep on going. Do not let it undermine your confidence. If you do, you probably will start to crumble, and then things will really go bad. If you can recover quickly and gracefully, you will earn your audience's loyalty.

An executive from a multinational food company was making a presentation to Wall Street analysts. As he discussed each of the company's products, a picture and brief description was displayed on an overhead projector. When he introduced the company's new line of frozen fried chicken, however, there was an obvious typographical error on the slide. It read, "Fried Children."

"Well, our new fried chicken is very popular with children," the executive said, not missing a beat. "Of course, we don't cook the children, just the chicken."

The audience chuckled, and the rest of his presentation went smoothly. While he acknowledged the error, he did not allow it to sidetrack the audience's attention or sabotage his presentation.

WASN'T THAT REFRESHING!

Over the years as a public speaker, I have encountered numerous "challenges" in front of audiences. I recall when I was addressing a distinguished group at the Toronto Board of Trade when suddenly my lapel microphone died. I stepped behind the podium to use the fixed mike. The podium, however, covered 75 percent of my body, which prevented the audience from seeing the gestures and body movements I was demonstrating.

One of the assistants rushed to my aid, bringing me a handheld microphone. Unfortunately, as she handed it to me, she knocked over a glass of ice water and completely doused my left side. Since I was behind the podium, the audience did not see a thing. However, they heard something, and when I stepped out from behind the podium they could see I was dripping wet on one side.

"As you can see, I'm a lot more refreshed and cooled off now," I quipped. Then, dripping and with ice in my shoes, I gave the rest of my presentation.

A BAD FACE DAY

I was invited to speak to a company that I had not worked with before. By 11:45 A.M., I was to be at the company and ready to begin a presentation at the stroke of noon. The company president was flying in for my program, which was to be no longer than 1 hour, and at 1 P.M. he was leaving on the corporate jet. Everything had been arranged, confirmed, and reconfirmed in advance.

At 8 A.M. I started to feel a throbbing pain on the right side of my mouth. By 9 A.M. it felt as if the right side of my mouth was inflamed. By 10 A.M. I knew that I was in trouble as the right side my face began to swell. As badly as I felt, there was no possibility of rescheduling. The CEO's administrative assistant had called me the day before, just to make sure that everything was "in order."

At 11:30 A.M. I was in the lobby of the company headquarters. The right side of my face was swollen like a balloon; my right eye was only a slit. When I walked into the auditorium to give my speech, I could hear the murmurs of shock. These people had never met me before, so they did not know what to expect.

And so I began my speech: "How many of you have ever had a bad hair day?" (Pause) "How many of you have ever had a bad face day?" I explained that I had an abscess in my tooth and that I would be in the dentist's chair at 2 P.M.

That was it! I launched into the rest of my presentation, never making another mention of the fact that I looked like a badly beaten prizefighter on the right side and a normal human being on the left. I won the respect of the audience. After my presentation, people came over to me and thanked me profusely. They told me they admired my courage.

As for me, it was liberating! Here I was, an image and communication specialist, and I had to give that speech looking the way I did. What it told me was that, as the presenter, I was secondary. My message was what mattered. I knew that, and the audience responded.

Gender Talk: Men and Women at Work

Jonathan and Diane are at a business meeting. They are equal in almost every way: position, expertise, professional experience, educational background, and intelligence. Despite these myriad similarities, chances are that Jonathan and Diane are very different in one critical area: the way in which they communicate.

Don't get me wrong. It is not that either Jonathan or Diane is better or more "correct" when it comes to communicating. However, if Jonathan and Diane exhibit the typical linguistic patterns of men and women in North America, they will have distinct communication styles. This will be exhibited in the way in which they speak to superiors, subordinates, and colleagues; how they discuss and evaluate their ideas; and how they react to criticism.

When discussing gender differences, it is necessary to generalize. On an individual level, you may exhibit all, some, or only a few of the attributes that are typical of your gender. Overall, however, the typical communication styles of men and women are very distinct.

Interestingly, *gender talk* is one of the most popular topics at my seminars. I believe that this is a direct reflection of the changes we have seen in the corporate world. Increasingly, corporations are opening more doors for women and developing their female talent. While women are still in the minority in the top ranks of corporations, there are notable exceptions. In the middle ranks, women are a growing force. The U.S. Bureau of Labor Statistics projects that by the year 2008, women will form 48 percent of the labor force, compared with 46 percent in 1998 and 25 percent in 1971.

The growing segment of female workers brings more women in contact with men (and vice versa). However, when women and men come together in business, this does not mean that they leave their gender differences at home. The problem, however, is that in our well-intentioned efforts to be politically correct, we may try to ignore gender differences in the workplace.

For example, during a recent seminar on creative coaching, which involved role-playing, participants were asked whether there was an obvious difference in the style of how men and women coached each other. Their response was quick. "No. We're all human beings." In dialogue afterward, however, there were noticeable differences in interpretations about what they actually observed between men and women.

To be an effective communicator, a fair-minded manager, a savvy entrepreneur, or a valued team player, you must recognize the ingrained communication styles of men and women (see Figure 8-1). With this understanding, you greatly enhance your ability to communicate successfully with others, and you will be able to hear, interpret, and understand others without judgment.

FROM THE PLAYGROUND

How we grew up, became socialized, and played with other children provided the foundation—often unconscious—of how we interact and communicate with others as adults. Deborah Tannen, a professor of

- Accept that there are differences in the way that men and women communicate. Be strategic in how you express yourself and more discerning in how you listen to others.
- Be more flexible. Learn to utilize a variety of communication techniques and styles to reach both men and women in your audience.
- Be aware of potential pitfalls of your own "gender talk."

Figure 8-1   Three reasons to become fluent in gender talk.

linguistics and an expert in gender differences in communication, undertook extensive research in the workplace. She found that the "ways of speaking learned in childhood affect judgments of competence and confidence, as well as who gets heard, who gets credit, and what gets done." These childhood communication patterns are reinforced by our interaction with our peers as we grow up. This is where the fundamental differences take root.

"The research of sociologists, anthropologists, and psychologists observing American children at play has shown that although both girls and boys find ways of creating rapport and negotiating status, girls tend to learn conversational rituals, whereas boys tend to learn rituals that focus on the status dimension," Tannen stated in an article in *Harvard Business Review*.[1] Thus girls learn to talk in ways that "balance their needs with those of others." Boys, on the other hand, tend to display their abilities and knowledge, "challenging others and resisting challenges."

Anyone who observes elementary schoolchildren can see these linguistic distinctions in practice. Girls learn from an early age how to build relationships, often by making others feel good about themselves and their abilities. If they are too aggressive or critical, they are labeled as bossy. Girls are rarely criticized by their peers for being too passive. Boys, on the other hand, challenge each other to determine the leader of the pack. A boy who is overly aggressive may be labeled a bully, but the bigger criticism among peers may be the accusation of being a weakling or a sissy.

> **Girls work to establish relationships with one another. As adult women, they tend to be more collaborative in the workplace, putting the relationship first. Boys challenge each other to establish who is going to be the leader. As adult men, they routinely challenge others and expect to be challenged.**

There are basic behavioral differences between men and women that continue through adult life. For example, women are usually more relationship-oriented than men. Therefore, if a woman is unhappy in a major relationship in her life, it usually will affect her ability to focus on her work. Men tend to be more defined by their status and derive personal satisfaction from what they do. Therefore, if a man is unhappy in his work, it usually will affect his ability to focus on his relationships.

These behavioral differences also can be observed when a man or a woman suddenly loses his or her job. For men, this can be extremely traumatic because they usually define themselves first by their titles and what they do for a living. I recall counseling a male executive in outplacement who insisted on meeting me offsite at a restaurant to brainstorm about how to market himself. The reason for this secrecy was that he was embarrassed and demoralized by being unemployed. In fact, he had waited 3 weeks before he had informed his wife.

While women are also traumatized by losing a job, they tend to see themselves in the context of a multitude of roles—wife, friend, mother, sister, caregiver, and so on. This helps to mitigate the negative impact of a job loss. This is not to say that a woman will not be affected when she is suddenly unemployed, but she deals with it differently, talking about it with her personal support network.

HE SAID, SHE SAID: COMMUNICATION STYLES

In a group setting, such as a staff meeting, men and women typically exhibit very different communication styles. However, this does not mean that one group has something more to say than the other; it is just different.

For example, in a general discussion, men tend to interrupt more. When they are speaking, however, they allow fewer interruptions. They also tend to speak more loudly when they feel they are not being heard. Women, on the other hand, interrupt others less and permit others to interrupt them. Not liking confrontation, women may even tolerate rude interruptions. Women expect to be invited to speak and tend to stand on ceremony. They are also more apt to seek permission to speak—often by raising their hands—in a group setting. In my seminars I tell women to abandon this submissive behavior and to learn to speak up.

Men usually speak in more of a monotone and typically use three tones of voice. Women vary their vocal quality more, using as many as five different tones—and women are also apt to sound more emotional at times.

Men make more declarative statements ("It's cold outside"), whereas women make more tentative statements with tag endings ("It's cold outside, isn't it?"). Men ask fewer questions to stimulate conversation and tend to lecture more. Women ask more questions to stimulate conversation and avoid lecturing in favor of give-and-take dialogue. Men disclose less personal information and are more to the point. Women disclose more personal information and tend to give too many details. Often they do not get to the point quickly enough.

Here's a workplace example of he said, she said communication styles in action. LeeAnn is a very competent professional, but when she speaks, she tends to provide too much detail. Her boss,

Ralph, can't understand why she won't just get to the point. Hearing so many words, Ralph tunes LeeAnn out. LeeAnn, sensing his distraction and impatience, provides even more details, begins speaking more quickly, and becomes even more long-winded as she starts to ramble.

HE SAID, SHE SAID: NONVERBAL COMMUNICATION

Men and women also differ when it comes to nonverbal communication, including eye contact, gestures, voice quality, and how closely they sit to another person (see Figures 8-2 and 8-3). As discussed in Chapter 6, your nonverbal communication will either enhance or contradict your spoken message. For women and men, therefore, it is vitally important to be aware of what your gender-specific nonverbal cues are saying about you. For men, body language that is too aggressive may make them seem combative rather than assertive. Conversely, if men use body language that is too passive, it may indicate weakness or boredom.

MEN
- Take up more physical space when sitting or standing.
- Tend to take more prominent positions in seating arrangements; e.g., the head of the table or closer proximity to the key decisions makers.
- Gesture away from the body.
- Assume more reclined positions when sitting and lean backward when listening.
- Use their arms independently from the trunk of their bodies.
- Invade others' personal space more often.
- Sit more at an angle and further apart from the other person, especially women.

WOMEN
- Take up less physical space, making themselves smaller by how they sit.
- Tend to observe the pecking order in seating arrangements before sitting.
- Gesture toward the body.
- Assume more forward positions when sitting and listening.
- Move their entire bodies as a whole.
- Provide more listener feedback through body language.
- Invade others' personal space less often.
- Sit directly in front of the other person, and sit closer to men.

Figure 8-2 Typical body language—men and women.

MEN

- Tend to avoid eye contact and do not look directly at the other person.
- Tend to angle their heads when listening.
- Often nod their heads to hurry another speaker along.
- Provide fewer facial expressions and fewer reactions in feedback.
- Exhibit less emotional warmth through facial expressions.
- Open their jaws less when speaking.
- Stare more in negative interaction.

WOMEN

- Look more directly at another person and make better eye contact.
- Nod excessively showing support to the point of submissiveness.
- Tilt their heads.
- Provide more facial expression in feedback and more reactions.
- Exhibit more emotional warmth through facial animation.
- Open jaws more when speaking.
- Avert gaze more in negative interaction.

Figure 8-3 Typical facial language—men and women.

For women, body language that is too passive may make them seem unsure of themselves and they will risk losing credibility. Conversely, if women use body language that is too aggressive, they may end up alienating others—especially female counterparts.

HE SAID, SHE SAID: HANDLING CRITICISM

Another essential difference in the communication styles of men and women is in the way in which they typically react to criticism. Learning not to take everything personally is a vital skill for women. For men, learning to deliver negative feedback diplomatically will improve their communication skills.

Diane works diligently on a report, staying late at the office on several occasions and going in on a Saturday. When she presents her report at a staff meeting, she hopes that it will reflect well on her. She is disappointed, therefore, when her boss does not compliment her. Instead of focusing on the positive, he dives into what's missing. "Can we get more market data?" he asks her. "Did you try talking to So-and-So?"

Jonathan, a trusted colleague at the meeting, raises questions about the conclusions Diane has drawn. When she explains, he challenges her further.

Diane leaves the meeting angry and hurt. Her boss's comments have shattered her self-esteem. As for Jonathan, she feels completely betrayed by him. When they leave the meeting, she gives him the cold shoulder and avoids speaking to him the rest of the day.

Consider the opposite scenario:

Jonathan works on a report, staying late at night and coming in on a Saturday. He presents his report at a meeting with his boss and colleagues. "There seem to be some gaps in the market data," his boss comments.

"That's the best I could find. Some market data are sketchy in some areas," Jonathan replies.

A male colleague challenges him, but Jonathan answers him point by point. The discussion becomes heated, but Jonathan holds his ground. His colleague, Diane, speaks up. "This report is the best documentation we've had on many of these markets. Like Jonathan says, the information in some of these areas is difficult to come by. Overall, though, I think this will be valuable to us moving forward."

At lunchtime Jonathan stops by the boss's office to see if he would like to grab a quick bite to eat. They are joined by the male colleague who challenged Jonathan at the meeting.

As these two hypothetical stories illustrate, women often find it more difficult than men to hear criticism. They are more apt to take negative comments personally. Men, on the other hand, tend to deal better with criticism because they expect to be challenged by other men. Men also have an easier time handling criticism and getting over it rather than brooding afterward. It is not uncommon for two male colleagues to get into a heated discussion in a meeting and then a short while later act as if nothing happened.

> **Women tend to be more sensitive to criticism and to transfer the information onto an emotional level. Men can direct "personal shots" or "digs" at each other in a meeting and yet walk out laughing together.**

For men, it may be enlightening to know that women do have a tendency to take feedback and criticism personally. Therefore, mentioning the good points—as well as the shortcomings—of her work will help her hear the feedback in a balanced way. Men need to acknowledge the positive first. However, if a positive is tagged immediately with a negative using the word *but*—for example, "That was a great job, *but* next time could you include more data"—women will tend to hear only the negative.

For women, it is important to keep in mind that men not only can handle verbal challenges, but they also expect and enjoy the verbal sparring. However, women also must realize that even though their male counterparts appear to be more resilient, they are more apt to bury their emotional reactions. They may feel angry or even hurt, but they are less likely to show it.

The other important lesson for a woman is that when it comes to criticism of her own work, she must understand that this is not a personal rejection. Admittedly, this is difficult. I can tell you from personal experience that when I first began presenting seminars, I was often taken aback when a man in the audience strongly disagreed with me or verbally challenged me. My immediate reaction was to take it personally. It took me a long time, but I realized that the best strategy was to thank the person for the candid comment and then explain my position. I realized that he was not trying to undermine my credibility or tear me down in front of others. He simply was telling the truth from his perspective.

Interestingly, when men challenged me, I found that they were usually very attentive when I explained my position. Women were less apt to challenge me. However, if they disagreed with what I said, I could see it clearly in their nonverbal cues (crossed arms, shaking their heads, rolling their eyes, etc.). It was only if I spoke up and addressed what I perceived to be their concerns that they responded. Otherwise, the women kept quiet about their negative opinions in public but would discuss it among themselves later.

HE SAID, SHE SAID: TAKING CREDIT

Raised to express themselves indirectly and to take a softer approach, women often use speech patterns that are more inclusive. This reflects their typically collaborative, relationship-building natures. When discussing a project in a group setting, for example, women tend to use the inclusive *we* more than the exclusive *I*.

Men tend to have more direct, pointed communication that is focused on a goal. Raised to think and act independently, they speak up for themselves at a young age. In business, when they talk, it is often to convey information and establish status—not to win friends.

Deborah Tannen refers to this gender behavior as "one up, one down." Language is used to establish a superior ("one up") or an inferior ("one down") position. "Men tend to be sensitive to the power dynamics of interaction, speaking in ways that position themselves as 'one up' and resisting being put in a 'one down' position by others. Women tend to react more strongly to the rapport dynamic, speaking in ways that save face for others and buffering statements that could be seen as putting others in a 'one down' position."[2]

Here's how the "one up, one down" scenario might be played out. Diane heads a team that launched a very successful initiative at work. Making her presentation to senior management, she uses inclusive language such as *we* and *us*. She even uses *we* when referring to parts of the project that she alone worked on. Drawing attention to her specific contributions runs contrary to her communication style. She is more focused on building rapport with her colleagues and sharing the glory than in drawing attention to herself. Her communication style is deeply rooted in her upbringing. As a youngster, Diane saw that girls who were too pushy or bossy were ridiculed and disliked by other girls. This is true in the corporate arena as well: One of women's biggest concerns is being called "bossy" or "tough."

Jonathan, too, heads a project at work. When he gives his report to senior management, he does give credit to the team and mentions some key players by name. When he discusses specific parts of the project that he handled, however, he switches to *I* in his presentation. This is comfortable for him because, as a boy, he was taught to use language to distinguish himself.

Both presentations are well received, but Jonathan and Diane leave distinct impressions. Diane does show that she is a team player and a project leader who values her team. By not taking credit for the project she spearheaded, though, she leaves some managers with the perception that she is not a major decision maker. Jonathan shows his strength, which may raise some managers' perceptions of him. However, he has to be careful not to appear to be tooting his own horn.

HE SAID, SHE SAID: IN CONVERSATION

Men and women are also very different in their conversational styles. Women tend to be more detailed and descriptive. When they relate a story or explain something, they start at the beginning and proceed to the end. In the extreme, however, a woman might come across as long-winded or lacking the confidence to discern the details and deliver the analysis. Men tend to be more blunt and concise. They aim for the bottom line as soon as possible. They may even start at the end and then relate the supporting details. In the extreme, however, a man could come across as lacking patience or even as being secretive and reluctant to share information.

Therapist and author John Gray discussed the different conversation styles of men and women in his book, *Men Are from Mars, Women Are from Venus.* While this book addresses personal relationships between the sexes, there are some interesting lessons to be learned about how men and women relate and process information. Gray writes:

> You see, men and women think and process information very differently. Women think out loud, sharing their processes of inner discovery with an interested listener. Even today a woman often discovers what she wants to say through the process of just talking. This process of just letting thoughts flow freely and expressing them out loud helps her tap into her intuition. This process is perfectly normal and especially necessary sometimes.
>
> But men process information very differently. Before they talk or respond, they first silently "mull over" or think about what they have heard or experienced. Internally and silently they figure out the most correct and useful response. They first formulate it inside and then express it.[3]

Men tend to avoid expressing their feelings of emotion or discomfort. Demanding an intimate conversation with a man might result in uneasiness, dismissal, or coldness. Women tend to be more open with their feelings and share personal information voluntarily. Women often derive personal satisfaction from taking relationships to a deeper level.

In a one-on-one conversation, a male and a female colleague may have a free and open discussion. Afterward, a woman may feel that her male counterpart understands her position and supports her. In a meeting with their boss and other colleagues, however, the man may not be as supportive of her as before. He may even sit back and let others challenge her instead of speaking up in her defense. When this occurs, women usually feel undermined or betrayed and cannot figure out the shift in their male colleague's behavior. The man, however, returned to his more natural way of communicating in the group dynamics. To his way of thinking, his colleague should have expected to be challenged. He does not see that he has been disloyal or unsupportive of his female colleague.

BREAKING THE STEREOTYPES

Stereotypes, we like to believe, are made to be broken. In an open, accepting society, we champion those who break through the barriers. But what happens when we meet someone who communicates in a way that is counter to our expectations? Reactions may range from surprise to mistrust to dislike.

Raj is a very gentle man from India. He meditates daily and practices yoga. When he speaks, he is very aware of others' feelings. At work, he often takes a collaborative approach. "What do you think about this?" he asks his direct reports. The problem, however, is that Raj's communication style runs counter to the typically direct approach taken by men in North America. As a result, Raj is seen as being tentative and lacking confidence. Understanding this, Raj has to work on being more direct in his communication without losing his gentle nature or his genuine concern for the thoughts and feelings of others.

Bev grew up a tomboy with five brothers. She learned at a young age that if she did not assert herself she would be left behind. In business, Bev maintains a no-nonsense attitude. She speaks her mind directly and has no problem asking for what she wants. While she is often viewed as "one of the boys," the men in her organization are not 100 percent comfortable with her.

To the women in her organization, Bev does not seem to be "one of them" or to champion them in business. Bottom line, they do not trust her and do not support her. Understanding this, Bev has to work on building her rapport with her female colleagues, learning to understand and appreciate the way they think and express themselves. Interestingly, women have been socialized to accept direct and even abrupt behavior from men, but they will rarely accept it from another woman.

If your communication style runs counter to the typical behavior of your gender, expect to meet with some surprise or resistance.

GENERAL PATTON AND THE SHRINKING VIOLET

When a person's communication style goes to the extreme of stereotypical behavior, another set of problems arises. Take, for example, the superdirect, aggressive "alpha male." This "General Patton" type may try to command respect but may end up alienating a large segment of the workforce. While the macho, directive-style management of the 1980s and early 1990s is out of date, there are still holdouts in the workforce today.

Doug was an ex-Marine who gave orders to the 80 women and 3 men reporting to him. Those who worked closest with him saw beyond the rough exterior. Once they got to know him, they discovered he was not a bad guy at all. The vast majority, however, resented his behavior. They felt bullied and belittled by him. Needless to say, morale in his department was low.

When Doug was told by top management that he had to change his manner, he was resistant to the idea at first. When I began to work with Doug, he told me that the way he spoke was just part of who he was. It was the way he was brought up. He was not sure that he could—or wanted to—act differently. Then one day I overhead him as he spoke to his wife on the phone. He was gentle and compassionate. He did as much listening as he did speaking.

With this insight, I helped Doug to understand the impact of his directness. The first step was for Doug to hear—from the source—how his communication style affected others. He sat down with the women on his staff and asked how he could give the feedback more effectively. They responded honestly. Doug had no idea that he was offending them. He committed to changing his approach, making suggestions instead of just making demands. Doug did not lose his firm demeanor, but he learned to tone down his macho direct approach with a more collaborative attitude.

Jen was smart and competent but had difficulty speaking up for herself. While she was liked by many colleagues, most did not recognize her abilities. When she dealt with more senior management, she was virtually invisible. This "shrinking violet" had such a low profile in her company that there was virtually no way she could be promoted. For Jen, "tooting her own horn" was completely distasteful and in conflict with the way she was raised.

Working with Jen, I helped her to realize that her submissive, indirect manner gave others the impression that she was ineffective and could not be taken seriously. First, she had to learn how to speak up, asking questions and making comments in meetings. She used social occasions at work, such a colleague's retirement luncheon, to allow others to get to know her and build a support network.

OUT TO LUNCH

For many men in the workplace, going out to lunch with a senior colleague or even the boss is easy and commonplace. Men have no problem seeking out a more senior person—someone who could potentially champion them in the organization. This is part of the "boys' club" that many men grow up with. Outside work, when they golf or have a beer together, they act as equals or peers regardless of their titles or salary levels.

Women, however, often do not choose to have that luxury. They may not see the value of having lunch with a colleague whom they find abrasive or do not particularly like. They also may feel self-conscious asking a more senior colleague or the boss to lunch. My advice to women is to go beyond "liking" or "disliking" someone. The business lunch is part of a strategy to build important relationships among colleagues. Women who feel excluded from the "boys' club" should jump on the bandwagon when it comes to lunchtime.

For example, if a woman has a proposal to present at an upcoming meeting, she would do well to build her support base in advance, talking to colleagues and getting their input. This helps ensure that when the proposal is brought before the group, she will have a supportive audience of both males and females. Men would do well to win over females by first establishing rapport with them. Women want to feel respected and valued for their knowledge. This provides the opportunity for both genders to establish a strong business relationship based on mutual respect. At no time should the business relationship take on an unwelcome, inappropriate overtone, such as with invasive personal questions. Permissible topics between business colleagues would include inquiries about one's children or one's home, such as renovations. Any topic that does not intrude into one's private life is fine (see Figure 8-4).

The tone and topics of conversations also must be addressed in male- and female-dominated environments. If you are among the gender majority, be careful that discussions are not geared toward only one group and that jokes or comments are not insensitive or offensive to others.

LEARNING FROM THE OTHER GENDER

By observing the communication styles and tendencies of your colleagues and others' reactions to them, you can learn valuable lessons. One of the most important insights is to see firsthand the kinds of behaviors and communication styles you *do not* want to adopt.

The differences in how men and women communicate mean that we can learn a lot from each other. The biggest lesson is to respect

Communication Don'ts for Men	Communication Don'ts for Women
■ Overly tough feedback with little sensitivity will make you seem like a bully.	■ Seeking instant approval when you put out an idea will undermine your authority and expertise.
■ Preaching or giving orders without experience or addressing the other person's need shows that you lack sensitivity.	■ Finishing your suggestions with tag questions such as "do you think?" will give others the impression you are less than confident.
■ Interrupting frequently or redirecting the conversation gives the impression that you are impatient and intolerant.	■ Ending your statements by raising your tone, as if you are asking a question, makes you seem unsure.
■ Avoiding eye contact or darting your eyes about while another is talking shows a lack of attention.	■ Standing on cermeony and waiting for the "most opportune time" to speak will make you seem tentative.
■ Speaking too quickly demonstrates impatience.	■ Being long-winded and too wordy shows indecisiveness.
■ Speaking in a condescending or patronizing tone—using words such as "should" or "must"—will put women off.	■ Speaking too quickly demonstrates nervousness.
■ Nodding excessively displays rudeness; you want the speaker to hurry up and finish.	■ Nodding excessively when someone else speaks implies submissiveness.

Figure 8-4   Communication don'ts for men and women.

the differences instead of judging only from your own perspective. When you allow yourself to walk in someone else's shoes, you are more likely to relate to them. How each gender responds to a situation is neither right nor wrong. This realization will only lead to win-win communication between men and women.

Developing Your Business Protocol Savvy

Business is not conducted only in the boardroom or your boss's office. In fact, you may meet your next important contact at a charity golf outing or a cocktail reception at an industry gathering. Mixing business and pleasure is standard practice and a valuable networking opportunity. This does not mean that you should bring your résumé to every dinner party you attend. But it does mean that you must develop what I call *business protocol savvy*—an essential set of skills for anyone, regardless of career or professional level. Your savvy includes the ability to greet and introduce others with poise, engage in casual small talk, and display impeccable manners at any business luncheon or dinner.

Think of it as the "finishing school" that every professional needs. This will give you the confidence and the knowledge of what to do when you enter a room full of people you do not know or when you suddenly find yourself standing next to the chairman of the board.

The two essential elements of business protocol savvy are discernment and decorum.

- *Discernment* is having the insight and judgment to act appropriately in any business/social situation.
- *Decorum* is conducting yourself with style and ease.

At this point you may be asking yourself if you *really* believe that table manners can make or break your career. To be truthful, most people would say no. Now consider the story of Henry. He was up for a promotion that would be the pinnacle of his career. His knowledge and experience were unparalleled, and he spoke five languages fluently. No one was better suited for the job from an expertise standpoint than Henry. He was flown to company headquarters to meet with the chief executive officer.

In the middle of the meeting, the CEO suggested that they take a break and get a bite to eat. Lunch was casual, and a few others joined them. What Henry did not realize, however, was that this luncheon had been arranged in advance to give other top executives a chance to meet him in a relaxed setting. It was really an extension of his interview. Unfortunately, Henry was not aware that he was actually on display. His table manners were atrocious. He ate hurriedly, with his head down, shoveling the food in. Then he slumped back in his chair, chewing on a toothpick. The other people at the table were completely turned off.

The word came down from above that Henry needed serious "polishing." He was a great candidate for the job, but the way he had acted reflected poorly on himself—and the company. He was called in by the head of his division and instructed to "clean up his act." This is where I came in. I booked several lunches with Henry and went through the ABCs of table manners and etiquette. By the end of our sessions, Henry had an etiquette toolkit that provided him with comfort and confidence. What Henry learned firsthand was that manners can open—or shut—doors of opportunity.

Good manners define you. They never go out of style.

ETIQUETTE FOR EVERY DAY

Your manners and the presence that you project will affect others' perceptions of you—whatever your position in the company. The rules of etiquette alone may not open the doors to the next level, but in order to be a viable candidate, you cannot overlook the importance of these softer skills. Even if you do not have ambitions to move up in the company, your ability to remain employable is enhanced by your business protocol savvy. When you know how to act and what to say, you boost your confidence for any business/social situation. Add to this the fact that so much of work today is team-oriented. In order to be a member of a team, you have to show respect for others and awareness of social conventions.

Etiquette is not old fashioned, nor is it reserved for afternoon high tea. Etiquette is a set of guidelines for everyday living. While the twenty-first century is the age of instant access—you can reach virtually anyone at any time and in any place—we cannot forgo the common courtesies of communication and personal contact. Granted, the business world, particularly in North America, has become increasingly casual. This does not mean, though, that basic respect and a sense of decorum are outmoded. In fact, in the last 5 years, I have seen an increase in requests for my business protocol seminars. The reason? There is a need to reinforce the rules of etiquette and social behaviors in a society where road rage, airport rage, and even cell phone rage have become all too common. Without guidelines for appropriate behavior, protocol goes out the window, and attitudes and actions become a free-for-all.

To distinguish yourself, become familiar with the basics of what I call the *etiquette toolkit.* Rather than focusing on obscure points such as the proper use of a fish knife, these rules will help you to polish your manners for everyday living.

YOUR ETIQUETTE TOOLKIT

- *Treat people equally.* Regardless of their profession or social status, treat everyone with the same respect and consideration. I have met businesspeople with impeccable boardroom manners who treat the waitstaff at a restaurant with rudeness and disdain. Service staff—whether in a hospital or a hotel—deserve your respect. Trying to prove your "superiority" by looking down on someone else will only succeed in putting you in a very bad light.

- *Arrive on time.* Keeping others waiting for you is rudeness in action. If you are delayed, let the other party know. Be honest when you estimate how long it will be before you arrive. Do not show up more than 15 minutes before your appointed time. If you do, you might appear to be disregarding the other person's time schedule.

- *Do not make others wait for you.* If someone arrives on time, do not make him or her wait longer than 5 minutes. If you are on the phone or if you have someone else in your office, explain that you have someone waiting and that you will get back to him or her by the end of the day. If there is an unexpected or unavoidable delay, then the least you can do is send someone else to explain the situation to your visitor.

- *Honor your commitments.* If you commit to doing something—whether a project at work or a social obligation—then follow through. If you break your commitments, your reputation will suffer. Why would someone trust you to keep your word in business if you brush him or her off in another situation?

- *Use diplomacy.* Diplomacy is the ability to say the truth without the sting. It is acknowledging another person's feelings and point of view when you have something difficult to say. Know when to speak up and when not to.

- *Know how to introduce yourself and others.* Next to public speaking, the biggest fear most people have is making introductions. They are afraid of messing up someone else's name—or even their own. A few simple rules will help: Look someone in the eye when you say your name—and smile. Both women and men should be comfortable shaking hands. Hold the other person's hand for as long as it takes to notice the color of his or her eyes.

- *Master small talk.* Good conversations are the framework for any business transaction. Small talk—light, casual conversation—helps to reveal your personality, warmth, sincerity, and sense of humor. The ability to make conversation is really an art that needs to be cultivated. Obvious topics to avoid in small talk include religion, abortion, politics, office gossip, race, and jokes with ethnic or sexual undertones. You may be an avid fan, but do not assume that everyone shares your interest in sports. Even if you do not have the "gift of gab," learn how to introduce yourself with ease and start a conversation. "What brings you here?" can be used as an opener in virtually any gathering where you find yourself next to a stranger.

- *Listen generously.* If you are engaged in a conversation with others, listen to what they have to say. The secret to good listening is to give of yourself. Put aside your own needs for a brief moment, and for the time they are speaking, make the other person feel like the most special person in the world. It is truly a leader who takes the initiative to make others feel comfortable. Do not just hear the words. Be an astute listener and observer of nonverbal communication. Make every endeavor to understand what the person is really trying to say.

- *Say "Please" and "Thank you."* These common courtesies demonstrate respect and recognize that you are asking for something, not demanding it. There is a world of difference for the listener between "Get me the file" and "Please get me the file." When a task is completed, a simple "Thank you" acknowledges the action. Your tone of voice in conversation also conveys genuine gratitude for what others say and do.

- *Send handwritten thank-you notes.* Never send a thank-you note via e-mail if you want the message to be meaningful. A personal, handwritten note is a courtesy that will make you memorable. A thank-you note need only be three lines: to express thanks, to acknowledge what was done, and to add something personal. Occasions for handwritten notes (preferably on personalized stationery) are birthdays, anniversaries, notable occasions such as promotions or receipt of an award, to acknowledge a gift, or to recognize someone's kindness and thoughtfulness. Thank-you notes also should be sent to the host within 5 days of attending a dinner or luncheon.

- *Give compliments sincerely.* Find time to recognize the efforts and actions of others. Tell them specifically why you are complimenting them: "Susan, you did a terrific job preparing that report. It is concise and factual, and you saved me hours of time." A natural compliment is never overdone or out of context.

- *Receive compliments graciously.* Tell the other person how the compliment made you feel. Express your appreciation. It is not vanity to accept and appreciate a compliment. It honors the person who gave it to you. Do not negate the compliment with false modesty: "The report wasn't that great." Why would you call into question another person's judgment? Do not automatically respond with a compliment in return.

Piggybacking off another compliment will dilute the impact of even a sincere comment. Wait until a more appropriate time to give someone else a compliment.

- *Act with integrity and authenticity.* This is at the heart of all appropriate behavior. Be sincere in what you say and what you do. Approach others with warmth and genuine interest in them. When you do, chances are that it will be reciprocated. Just knowing the rules of etiquette will not make you well mannered. Rather, you must respect yourself and others at all times.

Armed with your etiquette toolkit, you can tackle virtually any business/social situation. One of the most common is the cocktail party. This includes receptions that are held during industry conferences and sales meetings or even office parties.

THE BUSINESS COCKTAIL PARTY

Business and alcohol are a dangerous combination unless, of course, you use your head. The first thing about this type of gathering is that you do not go there to drink. You go there to meet others. Limit yourself to one or two drinks. Careers have been irreparably damaged by drunken behavior. I remember attending a cocktail reception years ago when one of the top executives drank so much that when he tried to sit down, he landed on the floor. He made such a fool of himself that no one who witnessed it—or heard about it—ever forgot it. If you feel more comfortable with a drink in your hand, then put ginger ale or mineral water in your glass. No one has to know what you're drinking.

The business cocktail party provides an opportunity to connect with a broad range of people. However, know that you—like everyone else—will be "on display" in a very public setting with people you know and do not know. Your behavior will be observed and critiqued, even if you are not aware of it. If you hate this type of event and do not want to play the game, then don't go. If you only show up to make an appearance, knock back a couple of drinks, and talk to one or two people you know, then you really aren't doing yourself any favors.

Know your real purpose in attending the event. Adopt a host mentality. Concentrate on making eye contact and greeting others with a sincere smile.

When you attend, make a real effort to meet other people. When you take the initiative to greet others and make them feel more comfortable, you are displaying the epitome of host behavior. Not only will you make a good impression, but the event also will be more meaningful for you. Do not look at others as strangers but as a potential connection waiting to be made. You may have to risk being rejected, which for all of us is one of the biggest fears, but when rapport is established and a business friendship begins, it is well worth the effort of taking the first step.

BREAKING THE ICE

The biggest challenge of the cocktail party is breaking the ice, particularly if it is an industry-wide function and you know few, if any, people there. One strategy is to position yourself near the door as if you are waiting for someone else. When a large group enters, join in with their walk. Do not barge into their conversation. Rather, use the comfort of this group to help you move into the room and begin to circulate. If you do not see someone you know, then look for other "white knuckled" drinkers standing alone and clutching their glasses. They generally are grateful for the company.

As you will recall from the etiquette toolkit, being able to meet and greet others and introduce yourself are essential skills. One thing to keep in mind as you mingle: Hold your glass in your left hand so that your right one isn't cold and clammy when you shake hands with someone. The handshake is the only physical contact you make in the business world. You want your handshake to convey confidence, competence, and approachability. No vice grips or dead fish please! Smile at the person and make eye contact. Be the first to volunteer your name. When the other person responds with his or her name, repeat it back to them. "It's a pleasure to meet you, John."

The moment you shake hands with someone, the clock starts ticking on the first impression you are making. Always stand when shaking hands regardless of gender. Introduce yourself first. Hold the other person's hand for a split second longer than duty requires.

Initiate conversation with a broad question: "What brings you to this conference?" Instead of asking the perfunctory, "What do you do for a living?" be more creative. One line that I often use to find out more about someone is, "How do you spend your leisure time?" This moves the other person out of business mode into another frame of mind. Have a 10-second "commercial" prepared about yourself. Instead of simply giving someone your job title, tell him or her what you do in a more engaging way. For example, instead of saying, "I'm the assistant director of research and development," you can describe yourself like this: "I help to develop the next generation of products for our company."

When making small talk, it is essential to be prepared on a number of topics. Read the newspaper before you arrive. Know what the stock market did that day. Be familiar with world news and current events. Stay away from topics that are politically controversial or negative in content. Ask others their opinions as opposed to standing on a soapbox. (For more tips on making small talk, see Figure 9-1.)

DO

Ask open-ended questions that encourage others to become actively involved in conversation.

Show genuine interest in the other person. Most people enjoy talking about themselves.

Ask questions that are relevant to the event or gathering, e.g., "What was your opinion of the keynote speaker at the conference today?" Or, "Have these networking events been useful to you?"

Know what tops the "headlines" of that day.

DON'T

Ask close-ended questions that can be answered by "yes" or "no."

Talk endlessly about yourself or lecture on your opinions.

Discuss politics, religion, or abortion, or tell off-color jokes.

Assume that everyone has the same interest in sports that you do, or shares the same team loyalties.

Figure 9-1   Do's and don'ts for making small talk.

EXCHANGING BUSINESS CARDS

Your business card is not to be given to everyone with whom you come into contact. Rather, wait until you have begun conversing and established rapport. Then ask the other person for his or her card. You now have permission to give the person your card. Looking at a card after it has been offered shows respect. If you are at a table, keep the person's card in front of you. If you are standing, the card can be put away after you have studied it for a few moments. For men, the card should go in the breast pocket of their suit jacket or sport coat, never in a wallet or back pocket. If you are not wearing a suit coat, put it in your shirt pocket. For women, invest in a cardholder, which you can carry in your purse or portfolio. Putting a card in a special holder shows that it is important to you.

Never jot down notes on another person's card, except for noting additional information, such as a home telephone number or an e-mail address. After the event, you may jot down notes in private on the back of the card.

Only give out business cards that are in excellent condition. Present your card with the letters facing the recipient.

The longest time you need to engage in conversation with someone at a networking event is 10 minutes. After that time, you may break graciously and circulate. One easy way is to say, "Will you excuse me? I see someone I need to speak to. We've been playing telephone tag for some time." Or "Thanks so much for talking with me. I've enjoyed our conversation." Don't say, "I'm going to get a drink." It would be impolite not to offer to get one for the other person. When you leave, move to another part of the room. Avoid the "window-shopper syndrome" of talking to someone, all the while looking to see who else is in the room. Do not give the impression that you are just biding your time until someone more important comes along.

When you are "working a room," you need to be standing. Others are far less apt to approach you if you are seated. As you circulate around the room, look for opportunities to join in a bigger group discussion. Do not try to edge yourself into a conversation between two people. They may be having a personal conversation. Position yourself just behind a group of three or more people who are having an easy conversation or simply standing together. If you catch someone's eye, smile. You will have a better chance of being invited to join their circle of conversation. In this way, you will not have to thrust yourself into the group with your hand extended as if you are canvassing for votes.

Another strategy is to stand near the hors d'oeuvre table or the dessert section of a buffet table. People tend to linger near the food. Recommending something tasty that you have tried is another good conversation starter. If you are at the end of the line for the buffet table, or if there is a long line at the bar, you have a captive audience. Commenting about the food, the parking situation, and so on (as long as you are not complaining) can be a conversation starter. Asking people what brings them to the event, how long they have been a member, and so on can be the basis of a quick conversation.

When you work a room, there may be people whom you really want to meet. For example, you might want to have some time with your boss or another executive. When you seek out these individuals, however, do not become glued to them. Remember the 10-minute maximum, unless, of course, your boss includes you in a larger conversation or wishes to introduce you to someone else.

Making introductions in a group involves a certain pecking order. The rule of thumb is to start with the most important person. Dignitaries take precedence over everyone—male or female—out of respect for their title and position: "Judge Connors, I'd like you to meet my boss, Sarah Jones. Sarah, this is Judge Franklin Connors of the Fifth District Court."

A customer would take precedence over your boss or a peer. Your introduction, therefore, would go something like this: "Sean, I'd like to introduce you to my colleague, Tom Smith. Tom is in charge of customer relations at the company. Tom, this is Sean Adams. He is the president of Adams & Associates, one of our newest customers on the East Coast."

When introducing two customers to each other, seniority comes first. Then age would dictate who is introduced first; always start with the oldest person. If everyone is roughly the same age, begin introductions with a woman. When you are at a business function, your boss would be introduced to others before your spouse or partner. However, in a purely social context—at a party, in an art gallery, and so forth—your spouse or partner would take precedence over a business associate. When introducing a couple, it is good to find out if the wife uses her own name. Or a couple may have professional titles that should be used when introducing them.

WHEN YOU CAN'T REMEMBER A NAME

It happens to all of us. You can't remember someone's name. For example, you are standing at a reception and a person stops to talk to you. You recognize the face but can't recall the name. The best strategy is simply to admit the memory lapse. "I'm having a mental block, what is your name again?" When you use the word *again,* it sounds as if it genuinely slipped your mind. For example, "Your name is on the tip of my tongue. What is it again?" With these simple phrases, you are taking responsibility without excessive apologies. Avoid saying, "I'm sorry I've forgotten your name." It may sound as if it wasn't important enough to remember in the first place.

Perhaps you see someone whose face is familiar, and that person is looking at you with the same "I have seen you somewhere" expression. Again, just admit the truth. "I know we've met recently. I certainly recognize you, but I'm bad with names." Then introduce yourself. This should prompt the other person to offer his or her name.

Here's another scenario: You are chatting with a colleague when someone who looks familiar stops to speak to you. You can't, however, recall the person's name. One solution is to inquire, "Do you two know each other?" Assuming that they do not, you can then suggest, "Please introduce yourselves." Should you wish to remove yourself totally from their presence and network with other people, casually say, "You two have a lot in common." They will naturally gravitate toward each other.

Everyone forgets a name on occasion. When it happens, don't be overly apologetic. Just admit the memory lapse, and ask the person for his or her name.

LEAVING FOR THE EVENING

If the reception was hosted by a particular person, or if you were invited by someone, then always seek out that person when you are leaving to thank him or her and bid farewell. Never be the last one to leave the cocktail party. You do not want to appear as if you have "closed down the bar." Remember, the "condition" in which you leave says as much about you as the presence you established when you arrived.

A brief handwritten note to someone you met at the reception— particularly if you had an extended conversation—will help enhance the impression that you made. Update your contacts with the names, phone numbers, and so on from the business cards that you have collected. Make note of any special interests or other particulars about these people. For example, let's say someone you met expressed an interest in a particular area of business, such as new wireless technology, or a hobby, such as deep-sea fishing or collecting antiques. If you come across an article on that topic, you can pass it along with a brief handwritten note. Look for ways to establish rapport and build a relationship.

THE BUSINESS LUNCH AND DINNER

The business lunch or dinner is another excellent way to socialize professionally. Entire books have been written on business etiquette, formal dining, and so forth. For our purposes here, I will focus on a few basic guidelines.

Guidelines for Business Lunches and Dinners

- *Be on time.* If you are the first to arrive, it is acceptable to wait for others in the front of the restaurant. Or if you are the first be seated at the table, alert the maitre d' that you are expecting guests. Stay away from ordering anything other than a cold beverage, such as sparkling water, but not alcohol. Otherwise, it gives the impression of being impatient.

- *No cell phones.* Turn off your cell phone when you are seated. If you are expecting an urgent call, you must explain the situation to the others at the table. If you do receive a call, excuse yourself from the table. Be as brief as possible.

- *Alcohol.* Alcohol at lunch is not desirable. The only possible exception is a glass of wine or beer, but only if you are having lunch with someone whose social style is to drink wine with meals. However, you are under no obligation to drink just because your guest or host does. If you wish, you may order sparkling water and drink it in a stemmed glass. At dinner, consume alcohol in moderation. One or two glasses of wine with a meal should be the maximum.

- *Ordering.* As a guest, ask the host what he or she recommends. The suggestions will give you some idea of the appropriate price points for the evening. Never order the most expensive or the least expensive dish on the menu. A mid-priced entrée is always in good taste. As a host, do your homework. Inquire beforehand what the specialties are so that you can make informed recommendations. If your guest orders an appetizer or a soup, you should as well so that he or she is not eating alone.

- *Prepaying the bill.* If you are hosting the luncheon or dinner, prepaying the bill is a courtesy that your guests will appreciate. Arrive at the restaurant ahead of time to make the payment and tipping arrangements on your credit card. In this way, when the meal is over, your guests do not have to wait. On the way out of the restaurant you can pick up your receipt or arrange to have it mailed to you. If you do not want to prepay, make sure that the waitstaff knows that the bill comes to you.

- *Formal dinner seating.* For a formal dinner, if there are no place cards, ask the host where you should be seated. The guest of honor always sits to the right of the host. Never take the place of honor unless you are specifically asked by the host.

MAKING CONVERSATION

Relationships in business are built on the golf course (or at sites of similar leisure activities) or around food. The business lunch and dinner are perfect opportunities to get to know someone and establish rapport beyond the typical "How is your day going?" If some business must be discussed or conducted, it should be done at the beginning or after the meal. Whenever possible, avoid business talk while people are eating the main course. Come prepared with three or four topics that would be of interest to the other guests, whether current events or the latest movies. Face-to-face interpersonal skills are no longer options for advancing your career. Being a skillful conversationalist lays the foundation for any relationship.

Do not underestimate the importance of small talk. It is only superficial when you do not take time to get to know someone.

DINING ETIQUETTE

Know the rules of dining etiquette. For example, the moment you sit down, your napkin goes in your lap. If you excuse yourself from the table, your napkin goes on your chair. At the end of the meal, your napkin should be folded and placed on the left side of your plate. However, it should never be placed on the table until all the plates have been removed from you and the other guests.

When passing the bread, serve the person on your right first. Do not serve yourself. Never cut a roll in half; always tear it into no more than two bite-size pieces at a time. Put enough butter on your plate that you do not have to "double dip." Always pass the salt and pepper together, even if someone asks only for one. Do not intercept anything as it is being passed. For example, if someone asks you to pass the butter to someone else, do not serve yourself before passing it on.

Eat easy foods. Avoid anything that is eaten with the fingers, such as chicken wings or corn on the cob. Do not order mouth-stretching triple-decker sandwiches or onion soup coated with gooey cheese.

If you are invited to a business dinner at someone's home—for example, your boss or a client—bring something to show your appreciation. Wine is often a good choice. Or you may bring a basket of cookies or a box of gourmet chocolates. Another option that I like is to send freshly cut flowers during the day so that they might be used as a centerpiece in the evening. Never bring flowers with you because it requires the host to leave the guests to attend to the flowers.

If you have any food allergies or dietary issues (e.g., you are a vegetarian), inform your host ahead of time so as not to appear rude if you avoid eating something. Never begin eating until the host sits down and invites you to begin.

"NET-IQUETTE"

The Internet, e-mail and even voice mail are important tools to stay in touch in business. However, instant communication has its potential drawbacks as well. (For an overview of business protocol tips, see Figure 9-2).

- *Cell phones.* Answering a cell phone when you are with someone else implies that they are not important. Do not expect others to wait for you while you are on a cell call. Refrain from using cell phones in restaurants or in meetings. Keep your cell conversations brief when you are in public. And never say anything that you would not want others to overhear. If you talk in public, they will hear it. Unless it is an emergency, do not ask to use someone else's cell phone. That person will have to pay for the call.

- *E-mail.* Respond to e-mail within 12 to 24 hours. If you are out of town, set up an "automatic reply" response to your e-mail. Use proper grammar, capitalization, and punctuation when writing e-mails. Never write in all caps; it will appear

- Avoid cell phone abuse. Give the people you're with your undivided attention.

- Introduce people to each other. Don't leave someone "standing there" without introducing him or her to others.

- Think before you eat. Even basic table etiquette will you define your level of professionalism in most dining situations.

- Don't be a "last call" drinker at the reception or cocktail party. The memory of your behavior will last longer in other people's minds than your hangover.

- Never send an e-mail in anger. Once it's gone, you can't retrace it, and the recipient can forward it at will.

- Stay away from gossip. Personal gossip, innuendoes, and other inappropriate topics of conversation could end up hurting someone else's reputation, and damage yours as well.

- Leave short, concise voicemail messages. If you always leave rambling messages, the listener will groan at the very sound of your voice.

- Honor other people's time. At a party or a reception where people are mingling, do not monopolize other people's attention. Heed the 10-minute rule, particularly if you are seeking out your boss or another senior executive. Any longer than that, and you may wear out your welcome.

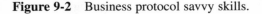

Figure 9-2 Business protocol savvy skills.

as if you are shouting. All messages, no matter how brief, should be clear, concise, and politically correct. Reread your message before you hit "Send." Once it is gone, you cannot get the e-mail back. Never compose or respond to an e-mail in a moment of anger. And do not send needless e-mails that you forward to everyone in your address book.

- *Voice mail.* When recording your voice mail greeting, smile as you speak and stand up to give yourself more energy. This will make you sound more personable and inviting. Keep your message simple and friendly. Do not make excuses or give multiple reasons why you are not there; simply state that you are unavailable to take the call. If appropriate, offer another contact person and phone number. Update your greeting daily if it outlines the days and times when you will be available. Return calls promptly, even if you do not have the resolution to the matter at hand. Keep others apprised of what is happening.

When leaving a voice mail message, keep it to a maximum of 30 seconds. If you have a lot of information to deliver, then talk in "bullet points." Speak slowly and clearly. Give your name and call-back number twice—at the beginning of the message and at the end—and say it slowly.

Companies seek out people who demonstrate leadership in business and who possess savvy in social situations. Those who excel at both will find that they are always in demand for business opportunities and social occasions as well.

The New IQ—Your
Inspirational Quotient

No man is an island; entire unto itself . . .
From "Meditation XVII," by John Donne, poet

For nine chapters I have discussed how to develop and promote your expertise and talents, how to build a professional network, and how to always put yourself in the best possible light. It is true that your opportunities for tomorrow will stem from how you invest in your career today. While the care and nurturing of your career are vital to your professional future, they cannot be your only goal. If they are, your satisfaction will be very fleeting.

Over the years, I have had the privilege of meeting many people who are successful by the standards of this world. They have position, power, and money. Some of them have attained levels of wealth and professional status that the rest of us only dream about. And yet I can tell you that their greatest satisfaction, personal joy, and sense of accomplishment do not come from the deals they have orchestrated, the amount of money they have earned, or the size of their estates.

Do not get me wrong. These people enjoy the financial fruits of their labors and all that goes with their success. But those who are truly wise understand one important thing: Nothing that they have acquired or attained can guarantee them happiness or insulate them from problems and worries. In this they are just like the rest of us. No matter what your position in life, the most enduring happiness does not come from what you do. Rather, it comes from what you do for others.

Knowing that you have made a difference to just one person carries an intrinsic reward. This is the kind of treasure that you store in your heart, not in your bank account. Neither time nor circumstances can tarnish this gold or ever take it away from you.

In this chapter I will focus on the three principles of your *inspirational quotient*. This new IQ reflects your capacity to inspire others. Regardless of your circumstances, level of achievement, or the amount of money you have, these three principles apply:

- Adopt an attitude of service.
- Find meaning in what you do every day.
- Show resilience in the face of adversity.

ADOPT AN ATTITUDE OF SERVICE

I remember when I first started out in this business. It took countless hours of networking to meet people, to "sell" my services, to build my client base, and to define my reputation. Over the years, I had the help and support of so many people—from friends who cheered me on to colleagues and other professionals who made introductions and opened doors for me. While I have been on the receiving end of such help, I have also made it a point to give it whenever and wherever I could.

And so it should be for you. While you are working to make connections, build your network, and capitalize on the opportunities that come your way, you must strive to be part of someone else's network. This can take many forms. Perhaps you have a particular expertise or level of experience that would be valuable in a mentoring program at your company or in your industry. Or you might have an "ear to the ground" for opportunities not only for yourself but also for acquaintances who are looking to change jobs—or find a new one. Just being available to listen to someone or to give them feedback is valuable.

You do not have to try to save the world. Rather, make it your goal to improve your small corner of it.

If you have achieved success, be an inspiration to others. If you found a particular industry group or business gathering to be a good source of job or client leads, then let others in on it. Invite a guest to the next networking opportunity. Keep in mind those talented colleagues and associates who would be of value to your employer. If nothing else, recruiting others will reflect well on you. Introduce someone around. Help him or her to make the next connection. However, be careful not to do this with a sense of charity. If you shepherd someone around because you feel sorry for him or her, you are not doing that person, or yourself, any favors. The other person may end up resenting your attitude, and you could come across as condescending. Encourage and help those whom you really believe in.

Never underestimate the value of listening. If you cannot offer job leads or recommendations to someone—perhaps you work in entirely different industries, such as pharmaceuticals and sporting goods—you can still help. Be a sounding board for someone else's ideas. Listen with an open mind. You do not have to have the answers, but your feedback may help someone to shape an action plan for the future. Read over a résumé, or critique a cover letter. These are seemingly small efforts that can be a big help. By giving of yourself, you show people that they—and their dreams and goals—are worthwhile.

Joseph is a success by anyone's measure. However, if you ever met my dear friend, you might not know just how successful he really is. A self-made man, he never "forgot where he came from," as the saying goes. More important, when he meets someone, he is far more interested in who they are—what they have to say, their views and opinions—than in talking about himself. What he gives to others is his genuine and sincere attention. He listens with an attentiveness that feels like a precious gift.

Your efforts to help do not have to cost you anything. The most valuable gifts you can give come from yourself— genuine concern, a listening ear, respectful feedback.

You also may choose to extend your help to others in far less fortunate circumstances. Through community or outreach groups, you can donate money and/or your time. Governmental budget cuts and the tightening of household purse strings have put a crimp in the funding of many charitable and social-services groups. You do not have to be a millionaire to adopt a philanthropist's attitude. It comes down to this: If you have the means, help out where you can.

My friend Jennifer volunteers at a soup kitchen for the homeless. Serving meals to those who are far less fortunate should be enough. But not for Jennifer. Her goal—her personal goal—is to serve these individuals as if they were in the best restaurants. For example, when Jennifer ladles out gravy on mashed potatoes, she is careful that nothing is spilled on the edge of the plate. Any drop is whisked away with a napkin. The extra care she takes is appreciated by those she serves. Because of a simple "Thanks," a smile, or a grateful look, she knows that her efforts do not go unnoticed. To Jennifer, she is serving much more than gravy. She is dishing out dignity.

FINDING MEANING

What do you *do*? If you are like most people, you have been asked this question millions of times. In casual conversation, the reply is usually a brief description of your job. However, this is not all that you do. Through your daily interactions in business and through your personal life as well, you touch countless people. When you can put your career into a bigger context, you can find meaning in any job.

Many jobs today are in the service sector. If this is where your career path has led, your daily job has a direct impact on the customer—an individual end user. It does not matter whether you work for a bank, an insurance company, a utility, or a retail chain, your efforts are all pointed toward anticipating and meeting the needs of the individual.

To find meaning in your professional life, look beyond what you do. Think about why you do it—and those who benefit. Putting a face on the job that you do personalizes it. Be like a doctor who does not think about practicing medicine but rather about making patients well.

The legendary Sam Walton, founder of Wal-Mart, spent his whole career in retailing, starting with his first Ben Franklin store franchise in 1945. He opened his first Wal-Mart in Rogers, Arkansas, in 1962.

"Once committed to discounting, Walton began a crusade that lasted the rest of his life: to drive costs out of the merchandising system wherever they lay—in the stores, in the manufacturers' profit margins and with the middleman—all in the service of driving prices down, down, down," *Time* magazine wrote as part of its "turn of the century" profiles of leaders of the twentieth century.[1]

Granted, Walton did become extremely wealthy through his Wal-Mart venture. According to *Time,* in 1985, the value of his Wal-Mart stock made him the wealthiest American at that time. While it is true that the Wal-Mart concept has been criticized and even vilified by traditional retailers, for Walton, the drive to discount has directly benefited cost-conscious consumers. Moreover, what set him apart was his conviction that every customer should be greeted as if he or she were a guest in his home.

If you only measure what you do by the paycheck you receive, you will never have "enough." Even if you become a millionaire, you will be dwarfed by the multimillionaire or the billionaire. The quest to acquire more will drive you ceaselessly. However, if you measure what you do by the difference you make every day—to your customers, your colleagues, and every person you come into contact with—then there will be no amount of money that can replicate the feeling of inner wealth.

Dr. Jane Goodall, the world's leading authority on chimpanzees and conservation, has launched a program called "Roots & Shoots" that aims to "empower young people all over the world who wish to make a difference."

In a PBS interview, Goodall explained the program:

> Roots & Shoots is about making the world a better place for your own human community, for animals, including domestic animals, and for the environment that we all share. And its most important message is that you as an individual make a difference. You matter. What you do today actually affects the situation in the world, and it is hard for adults, particularly, to realize that in a world of 6 billion plus people, individual action actually does make a difference. Children understand that more readily.[2]

But what about you? In your day-to-day job, the nine-to-five world that most of us occupy, can you make a difference? Or do you have to be a millionaire or someone famous to really make a difference?

Throughout my career I have met individuals from every possible profession—from academics to sales executives, researchers to bankers—who made it their purpose to make a difference by what they did. Their attitudes have inspired me and refocused my priorities. These attitudes can be condensed into some basic rules to follow:

- Understand the impact of what you do on those you touch directly, whether your customer is an individual, a company, or a community.
- Strive to make your daily work as personal as possible to you, your colleagues, and the customers or clients whom you serve.
- Put a human touch into your daily interaction from the simple "Please" and "Thank you" to notes of encouragement.
- Give hope to others by your attitude and actions.

Maya Angelou has devoted her life and her writings to inspiring people to overcome prejudice, discrimination, and abuse. As the National Women's Hall of Fame notes, "Angelou's writings have altered society for the better, bringing greater diversity into the theater and literature. Her autobiographical works provide powerful insights into the evolution of black women in the twentieth century." Her personal story of triumph has moved all of us to expect more of ourselves and of others. Through her words, she has given us hope.

SHOW RESILIENCY

No one lives a charmed life. No matter how fancy the car, how big the mansion, how opulent the lifestyle, everyone has their share of problems and sorrows. You will not be spared, nor will I. When you encounter misfortune—professional, financial, or personal—your only tool is resiliency. It is a powerful force that only you can give to yourself.

Resiliency is sometimes defined as "irrepressible liveliness and good spirit." Think of it as picking yourself up out of the emotional mud, wiping off the mess, and moving on.

In a recent *Harvard Business Review* article entitled, "How Resilience Works," Diane L. Coutu writes, "We have all seen it happen: One person cannot seem to get the confidence back after a layoff; another, persistently depressed, takes a few years off from life after her divorce . . . What exactly is that quality of resilience that carries people through life?"[3]

With resilience comes the strength to move on—in the middle of or despite difficulties, challenges, and even traumas. Moreover, resilience allows us to find meaning and lessons in the midst of the crisis.

"This dynamic of meaning making is, most researchers agree, the way resilient people build bridges from present-day hardships to a fuller, better constructed future. Those bridges make the present manageable, for a lack of a better word, removing the sense that the present is overwhelming," Coutu writes.

One of the "building blocks" of resilience, she adds, is the ability to "make do with whatever is at hand." I have seen so many examples of this in my own life and in the lives of those with whom I have worked. When a person can accept the current circumstances—be it demotion or termination—this greatly increases his or her chances of overcoming this immediate difficulty. However, when a person wallows in self-pity, denial, or blame, it only extends the painful period. It is impossible to move on when clinging to the negativity of the past.

To move up, move ahead, or move on, you must stop dwelling on what did not happen or what should have happened. Look at your current circumstances. Even the tiniest glimmer of hope can become a beacon if you focus enough attention on it.

In the midst of writing this book, my husband, Vince Settineri, died suddenly. I cannot tell you the pain and shock that I felt. He had not been feeling well for a few months, but no one—not even I—had any idea. I frantically drove Vince to the hospital at 7:45 on a Saturday night when he began having severe chest pains. Soon after, he was pronounced dead. I begged the doctors to bring him back to life. They told me that there was no hope. The love of my life took his last breath at 8:20 P.M. on August 31, 2002. He was here, and then he was gone.

Before Vince's death, I thought I was living a charmed life. I had a successful career doing what I loved. I had a warm and close relationship with my son, Sean. I was surrounded by loving family and friends. And I had the unconditional love and support of my husband, whom I adored. Then my world caved in.

All the resilience I could muster could not fill this void. I was blessed with the loving support of family and friends and many amazing clients to help me get through. Having a business to run also brought structure and purpose into my life. Vince, a successful businessman, understood very well the importance of keeping one's commitments and of a job done well with purpose and integrity. I kept busy, and I moved ahead.

What has helped me to continue through this difficult period of my life are the three principles: helping others, finding meaning, and resilience. Each day I recommit myself to them. These principles will not just help you get through. I believe that they have the power to help you to get beyond yourself, your circumstances, and whatever pain or fear you are facing.

A DOSE OF GRATITUDE

There is another ingredient in your inspirational quotient—gratitude. This feeling of thankfulness is the great equalizer when you are feeling the high highs as well as the low lows. Gratitude leads you to acknowledge that your success does not belong to you alone. Perhaps you assign a spiritual meaning to it. Or you may see your success and good fortune in the context of the support, love, and encouragement you have received over the years. Gratitude does not take away anything from you. Indeed, I believe that it increases the joy you can gain from your success and good fortune.

Adopt an *attitude of gratitude*. It increases the joy when things are good. It lessens the pain when things do not go your way.

Gratitude also helps you to keep perspective when you are faced with adversity. You may have lost out on that job, promotion, or major client contract, but you can still be grateful for the family, friends, and loved ones who are part of your life. You may suffer a personal loss due to illness, death, or another tragedy. Be grateful for the others around you and a job that gives structure and meaning to your life.

Your inspirational quotient is not a prescription for rose-colored glasses. On the contrary, it is a big dose of reality. Your inspirational quotient increases when you can accept things just the way they are and still move forward. From this perspective, you can become the person on whom someone else can lean or rely when difficulties arise. Just as you have a professional network for business opportunity, you must be part of a *resiliency circle* of close family and friends. Be there for each other when things are good—and when they are not so good.

If there is one important lesson to take away from this book, it is that you have power as an individual. That power is magnified when you participate in a healthy and symbiotic network of other individuals. The source of it, however, is you.

There is no magic formula for success. There is no shortcut on the road to riches. There is only you. Your authenticity, integrity, talent, expertise, personal conviction, and caring are all you ever have—and all you will ever need.

In an uncertain business world, this is the reality. It is also the hope that most of us need. Your future is not decided by someone else.

The decision makers do not have your fate in their hands. By taking responsibility for your professional life, you also take charge of it. It is the true meaning of that old adage about "taking lemons and making lemonade."

Diane Coutu in *How Resilience Works* refers to this ingenuity as "bricolage," which "in the modern sense can be defined as a kind of inventiveness, an ability to improvise a solution to a problem without proper or obvious tools or materials."[4]

The successful professionals and entrepreneurs with whom I have worked over the years have had this kind of inventive skill. They took the odds and ends of opportunities, added a bit of luck and the force of sheer determination, and forged their own futures. Yes, circumstances do play a part. But it is your attitude that is the determining factor between circumstances that pay off and those that do not.

I remember sitting on a bus in Toronto so many, many years ago and dreaming about the business I would start. The ideas came together as image and communication. The road from then to now has been very long and often bumpy (and sometimes scary), but I have been blessed with a certain kind of inventiveness that has allowed me to forge my talents, abilities, and interests into a viable business. The other component was a healthy bit of fear: When used properly, fear is a great motivator. By this I do not mean fear of the paralyzing variety. Rather, the fear I speak of is the realization that unless you take some action, things will not get any better by themselves.

You alone are in charge of your destiny, but thankfully, you are not in it alone. To start this process today, here are five simple steps you can take:

1. Call or write a business friend and schedule a lunch to catch up. Find out if there is a potential networking opportunity.

2. Call a friend whom you know has been looking for work or trying to change jobs. Offer a word of encouragement or any ideas that you might have.

3. Renew a relationship with a mentor or coach. Ask yourself, "Who are my teachers today? Who is the first person I would call for career advice?" Look for people whose wisdom and personal counsel you value.

4. Find your most recent annual performance review and read it thoroughly. What action plans were outlined or hinted at that you can use as a springboard to action.

5. Make it a point to get up from your desk, out of your work space, and away from your phone to talk with other people outside your department. Commit yourself to using host behavior to experience your current situation differently.

BUILDING YOUR CONFIDENCE

As you define your purpose and intentions, you will gain more confidence in your career and life choices. When you have confidence in yourself and your ideas, others will as well. If you like the person you are, others will. If you believe that you can get the job done, others will.

Today more than ever, companies are looking for good people—whether employees or consultants—who can get the job done without the added burden of emotional baggage and negative energy. Meeting project milestones and ensuring that deliverables are accomplished on time and on budget are great ways to build your credibility. Speaking the truth diplomatically sends the indelible message that you are true to your values and that you have the best interests of the organization at heart.

When you can step back from an opportunity because you know someone else is better suited, you demonstrate your commitment to high-quality teams. When you champion someone else, you show your true leadership. Ask yourself, "What is best for the company, what is best for my team, and what is best for me?" These are the criteria by which your decisions should be made. If you do, you will find that others will respect your choices and support you in the tough spots.

STATE OF BEING

There is another important element to natural leadership, and that is a sense of optimism. People are attracted to what is celebrated. Optimistic leaders always seem to have something to celebrate or some positive occurrence to discuss. It is not that they overlook the negative, the difficult, the challenging, or the traumatic. They have learned, however, that nothing is 100 percent without hope.

Optimists are positive about themselves, their abilities, and accomplishing their goals. However, they are still realists, seeing the world as it is. They know what options are available to achieve their goals. When difficulties arise, they discuss them in a realistic fashion—but with optimism. They always believe that there is a solution. They seldom take the entire blame on themselves. By externalizing negative situations, they are less affected personally so that they are empowered to be part of the solution. They get ahead because their belief systems allow no alternative.

Set goals, and celebrate when you achieve them. There is nothing better to lighten your mood and the mood of those around you than a good celebration.

BEING HUMAN

Allow people to connect to you on an emotional level while still honoring your leadership. Admittedly, this is a thin line to walk. You want others to perceive you as competent and in control of your destiny, but this can intimidate some people. Soften it by allowing some of your foibles and faults to show so that people see you as human instead of as a driven perfectionist. Be vulnerable at times. Share appropriate anecdotes that illustrate some of the hard knocks and challenges you have dealt with in getting where you are with others. Talk about what makes you happy about your work. Let your enthusiasm shine through.

Few people enjoy dealing with someone who is always serious or who takes personal responsibility for everything that happens. Know when it is time to share in or create some fun and when it is time to work. For example, be able to joke with members of your team while still getting down to the business at hand. This is an integral part of the quality of work life that most people seek. Remember that old saying in sales, "People don't care how much you know until they know how much you care."

Know, too, that humility is a virtue. As much as you have to believe in yourself and the value that you bring, you also must act humbly. True humility has a spiritual quality to it, acknowledging that your success is due, in part, to the efforts of others. A humble attitude also invites others to relate to you on purely human level.

If you can pick one thing to improve on every day, let it be the ability to get along with the people around you. No other quality or ability will take you farther or get you more notice.

I am convinced that people are awarded projects and job responsibilities based on their ability to get along with others. In my own career, my clients have engaged my services, I believe, because they find me to be credible, and they like what they see/hear/feel in our first meeting. The repeat business that I have enjoyed from clients is a direct result of liking what I do. Without the initial "like who they meet" phase, though, I could never get to the "like what I do" stage with my clients. And for this I am eternally grateful.

PRIORITIES AND TRADEOFFS

While the focus for so many people today is on their professional lives, it is necessary to keep a balance. Your personal life and your work must reflect both your priorities and tradeoffs. Otherwise, you waste your most valuable currency—time. To do this, you must undergo a "heart checkup." When was the last time you had a real life priorities conversation or a heart-to-heart conversation with someone close to you? Think about your friendships. When was the last time you asked someone how he or she was and stopped what you were doing long enough to hear the answer? Are you worried that you and your partner do not talk anymore? Scheduling a "heart checkup" with someone close to you can help address these matters.

When you have a greater balance between the personal and professional aspects of your life, you will lessen the feeling that you are sacrificing one part of your life for the sake of the other. When you are at work, you will worry less about home. When you are at home, you will think less about work. This is not to say that you will not be faced with tradeoffs and priorities constantly. They are a fact of our modern working life. Over time, however, you will see the priority setting and tradeoffs as integral to your life and career plans.

Another way in which to enhance the satisfaction you gain from your career that also will benefit the personal areas of your life is an attitude of lifelong learning. Are you learning something new? Do you have another accomplishment to acknowledge? Have you helped someone else be more successful in the execution of his or her day-to-day responsibilities?

There is so much more to life than just a job. Are you using your job to realize other personal goals, such as service to others, professional growth, or building a strong and resilient network of supportive peers?

What do you need to feel successful at the end of every day?

DO WHAT YOU LOVE

Are you doing what you love? If not, consider career counseling to help you find what will make you truly happy. If you feel burned out, you may not be doing what you really love and may need to reinvent your job. If you feel rusted out, you may not be using your talents and abilities to their fullest potential. If you are doing what you love to do, are you moving forward along your chosen path?

To enable greater growth in your professional life, consider these steps:

1. Look at what is required in your current job responsibilities and where you want to be next. Map out a learning plan and review it every 3 months.

2. Talk to people about your career aspirations, especially those who work in the area or field that most interests you. If people know you are interested, they are more apt to call you first if an opportunity arises.

3. Read, read, read. Subscribe to magazines and industry periodicals that give perspective on trends in your area of expertise, organizational development, and industry in general. Ask yourself, "How can I apply this knowledge in my current situation?"

4. Join professional associations so that you can find out what people in other industries are doing. Build a network of people who look to you as an expert in your field.

5. Share your intellectual property freely. There is no value in possessing great knowledge if no one knows about it.

6. Every day ask yourself, "What did I do to get better and to stretch beyond my limits?"

Taking steps to move yourself continually forward will help you to feel more in control of your life, particularly when faced with an unplanned detour or setback. As Mike Lipkin writes in his book, *Your Personal Best,* when life seems unfair, you have two basic choices.

On the one hand, you can obsess about how you won the race but did not get the prize and blame and punish all those whom you think betrayed you. Or you can accept that you have just been through an experience that was waiting to happen.

As Lipkin writes:

Life is all about crises. Some are big and some are small, but it's your ability to resolve them that ultimately determines whether you live at YOUR PERSONAL BEST. And the more successful you become, the more crises you will have . . . Know that crises are merely milestones, along the path of destiny. You control your destiny by the way in which you handle each crisis.[5]

He continues:

If you believe that you are in control of your own destiny, you automatically take personal responsibility for everything that happens to you. You hold yourself accountable to yourself. You're autonomous. You know that happiness is an inside job . . . You know that you can influence all the most important things in your life, including the attitude with which you accept those things that you cannot change.[6]

Above all, do not wait for life to happen. It already did. If you judge yourself against other people, you are setting yourself up for discontent. If you live in the shadow of others, you will pale by comparison. To thrive, act like you have won the lottery, smile like you are in love, and live like today is a new beginning. Life offers no shortcuts or guarantees. Take your life experiences and transform them into successes by seeing the lessons they contain.

Tomorrow is uncertain. While the past is not forgotten, it is today that will define my destiny. Vince taught me that memories, courage, gratitude, and faith will shield me from the unknown. And I know that I am not alone on my journey, for I have you, my friend, to share in the present.

Epilogue

THE NEW PIONEER SPIRIT

One thing is certain: Things will always change. Opportunities arise. Choices are made. Options narrow. Scopes broaden. Jobs are eliminated. Positions are created. Priorities are reordered. In other words, life happens.

Against this backdrop of constant change, you draw your career path. From the starting point of where you are—whether recent college graduate, seasoned professional, employee in transition, or entrepreneur—you target where you want to be. The distance between these two points is where your career path leads. But this pathway is not set in stone; rather, it is etched in sand. It is shifting constantly. What you thought you wanted 5 years ago may not be what you want now. What you thought was available 5 years ago may not be available now.

Thus, to effectively customize your career, you must harness two powerful and sometimes contrary forces. One is what you want. The other is external change. If these forces are diametrically opposed, you probably will stay stuck, making no headway. By working with both forces, however, you can move in new directions.

Kim had a successful career selling media advertising and in the 1980s was enjoying a six-figure income. While she liked what she did well enough and certainly felt rewarded for it, Kim knew that she could not do it forever. The career path dictated by her true talent—the deep desire of her heart—was interior design. There was no way her current career path was going to lead to that goal, so Kim shifted courses dramatically. She quit her job and took a $30,000 position while she studied interior design. She knew that she had the talent. What she needed was the opportunity to make things happen. Kim's dedication to her vision paid off. Today she is a highly respected designer working with commercial and residential clients. With her background in sales and a strong customer focus, Kim decorates based on the client's lifestyle and needs. By daring to view her career in a different way, Kim customized her professional future.

Pat started out as a sales representative in the field in a territory he had all to himself. As the company grew and added more product lines, however, it also added more sales reps. In time, Pat was not alone in the territory. He had colleagues calling on his customers, albeit with different product lines. If another sales rep had a problem with a customer, Pat had to fix it.

Circumstances had obviously changed, leaving Pat with two choices: Leave the company or adapt to the team approach. In the end, Pat chose to stay in sales and adapt. Importantly, Pat's decision was not based on fear of not being able to get another job. Rather, it was based on the fact that he loved sales and believed that he could make a difference by staying with the company. In this way, Pat customized his career.

For both Kim and Pat, while their professional circumstances were very different, they have one important commonality: They operated from the basis of their true purpose, following their gut and their heart. Each had a specific goal in mind and worked to fulfill it. So, too, it is with you. As you move forward, you have an important guide—your personal mission statement. This statement, as explained in Chapter 1, embodies your purpose; the deployment of your talent, experience, and abilities; and the end result that you wish to achieve. Your personal mission statement motivates you, steering you along a specific path. At the same time, it is the gauge by which you evaluate any opportunity or decision to see if it brings you closer or takes you away from a desired outcome.

As you grow and change and develop your true talents, your mission statement should reflect that growth and maturity. The way you see yourself and your purpose at age 25 may not be the same at age 35 or age 45. And by age 55, after a 30-year career, it may be very, very different.

In order to accept the change that inevitably will come into your life, you must learn when to let go. It is not that you ignore the past or its lessons. In fact, you should embrace them because those experiences brought you to the present. However, you cannot reshape the present to match the past. It can't be done, and you will waste all your time and effort on a futile endeavor.

Sadly, many people today have gotten so caught up in the way things used to be. The decline in the stock market and the economic and geopolitical uncertainties cloud their vision and alter their perspective. Able to see only what has been lost, they are in a state of mourning. They remain victims, unable to move up, move ahead, or move on.

THE NEW PIONEERS

Those who adapt have a pioneer spirit. They learn from the past but are not held back by it. They view the business world as totally transformed and accept that, for better or worse, things will never be the same again. They learn to trust change and to let go of expectations of the past. Moving ahead, they surround themselves with positive energy and like-minded people. Moving up, they do not fight the impossible but learn to channel the forces of change. Moving on, they are creative, always looking for the opportunity that they did not see before.

Adam worked in the creative department of a large public relations agency for years. His wife worked in the same agency, but in a different department. As Adam's career hit a plateau, his wife's skyrocketed. As she was being groomed to become the head of her department, Adam realized that he had gone as far as he could go. Instead of feeling victimized or, worse yet, resenting his wife's success, Adam became revitalized with the prospect of change. He saw opportunities everywhere and pursued every one of them. He was not disheartened when things did not pan out. Rather, he saw it all as part of the process of elimination that would lead to the best place for him. As I write this, Adam has just landed a new job, an opportunity he was not even aware of 1 year ago.

In this new pioneer spirit, people are shedding limited and preconceived notions of themselves and the opportunities available to them. Just recently a woman spoke up in one of my seminars. For 20 years, she admitted, she rarely said much in large gatherings. In a group meeting or conference, she would listen attentively but did not add to the discussion. Her communication was limited to one-on-one dialogue. In the seminar, however, she spoke up. She admitted that her reticence to speak had to do with the way she was raised and her father's opinion that women should be quiet and submissive.

"But that's not the way it is now," she told her colleagues at the seminar. "It's time to move on and take control of my life and my future."

Her colleagues gave her a standing ovation.

Everywhere you look there are people just like you who are blazing new trails. Like you, they recognize the need to customize their careers, to assess where they are, and to identify where they want to be. It is not just the high achievers or those on the fast track who are customizing their careers. On the contrary, this process is vitally important for the person who is starting out, for the person who has just been laid off, and for the person who is changing careers at midlife. The only difference between the person at the top of the career ladder and the person at the bottom is how much they believe in their own gifts and ideas.

To begin today and to continue into the future, you need to follow an ongoing process to customize your career. Here is a summary of the steps:

1. *Evaluate your personal mission statement.* This is a living document that should identify your desired goal and help you to take the steps to reach it.

2. *Be true to your true talents.* If your natural gifts are not a focal point of your career, then you must make a change.

3. *Surround yourself with people who will champion you, particularly when others are saying "no."* This includes coaches, mentors, role models, and good friends.

4. *Adopt an attitude of gratitude and true humility.* No one gets ahead without the help of others and without helping others.

5. *Look at failure as an opportunity to get a free education.* Learn how to rise above the obstacles.

6. *Take time to celebrate all the small things.* Your character is not defined during the happy times but rather during those times when the roadblocks seem permanent.

7. *Do not set unrealistically high expectations so that you become disheartened.* Do not set such low expectations that they are meaningless.

8. *Leave a legacy that honors you as a person, a friend, a loved one, a parent, a colleague, a humanitarian, or a community member.* If you only measure yourself by the money you make and your job title, you will always shortchange your fulfillment.

To customize your career, you must live fully in the present, learn from the past, and have positive expectations about the future. Some things will not turn out as you plan. You will face setbacks. You will lose out at times, and sometimes you will win when you least expect it. But if you are fully engaged in your life, with a personal mission, a plan, and the drive to achieve your goals, you will vastly improve your chance for success. More important, you will have a more fulfilling journey and be in control of your own life.

Endnotes

Chapter 4

1. Malcolm Gladwell, "The New-Boy Network: What Do Job Interviews Really Tell Us," *New Yorker,* May 29, 2000.

2. Teri Agins and Lisa Vickery, "Heads Up—The Suits Are Coming: Casual Wear for the Office Is Still In, But Dressing Up Is Creeping Back in Style," *Wall Street Journal,* April 26, 2001.

Chapter 6

1. David Pringle, "Career Journal: Learning Gurus Adapt to Escape Corporate Axes," *Wall Street Journal,* January 7, 2003.

Chapter 7

1. James Gray, "Take a Tip from How Kids Talk," *Globe and Mirror* (Toronto), November 29, 2002.

2. Granville N. Toogood, *The Articulate Executive: Learn to Look, Act, and Sound Like a Leader* (New York: McGraw-Hill, 1995).

Chapter 8

1. Deborah Tannen, "The Power of Talk: Who Gets Heard and Why," *Harvard Business Review,* September-October 1995, p. 140.

2. Ibid., p. 141.

3. John Gray, *Men Are From Mars, Women Are From Venus* (New York: HarperCollins Publishers, 1992), pp. 67-68.

Chapter 10

1. John Huey, "Discounting Dynamo, Sam Walton," Time.com (http://www.time.com/time/time100/builder/profile/walton.html).

2. PBS interview, "Jane Goodall on Finding Your Purpose," http://www.pbs.org/kcet/globaltribe/voices/voi_goodall.html.

3. Diane Coutu, "How Resilience Works," *Harvard Business Review*, HBR at Large, September 2002, p. 2.

4. Ibid., p. 5.

5. Lipkin, Mike, *Your Personal Best: The 12 Personal Best Practices to Help You Live at Your Highest Level*, (Environics/Lipkin, 2002), p. 78.

6. Ibid., p. 78.

Index

Note: Boldface numbers indicate illustrations.

A

abilities, 2, 39–41
accepting responsibility, 110–111
adventurousness, 9–10
aggressive behaviors, gender
    differences in communication
    and, 160–161
alcoholic consumption, etiquette
    and protocol in, 178–179
Angelou, Maya, 191
Ansell, Jeff, 121, 140
appearance, dress, 22, 52–53,
    58–59
  "bad face day" and, 145–146
  casual dress in, 64, 67
  consistency in, 62–63, 62
  corporate casual attire in, 66–67
  corporate formal attire in, 66
  expectation and, power of, 58–59

first impressions and, 53–58
fit in, stand out, 59–61
four categories of business attire
    in, 66–67
image and, 51–58, 61–62
image makeovers and, 67–69
looking the part and, 63–65
middle casual attire in, 67
over- vs. underdressing, 63–64
positive vs. negative self-image
    in, 58–59
presence in, 57
relaxed casual attire in, 67
self-image and, 58–59
statement made by appearance
    and, 65–66
Twelve B's of, **63**
visual impact in, 57, **58**
Articulate Executive, The, 133
assessment (*See also* internal
    assessment), 10, 15–16,
    23, 48
attitude, 22, 52–53

attitude of service, 186–189
audience for presentations, 121,
    121, 124
audiovisual aids for presentations,
    133–135

B

"bad face day," 145–146
baseball technique, 140
beginning with the end in mind,
    6–8
body language, body postures,
    81–85
    gender differences in
      communication and, 152–153,
      152, 153
    listening skills and, 106–107
Bottom Line Personal, 9
"bricolage," 195
building your life raft ahead of time
    using networking, 93–94
building your professional circle
    (*See also* networking),
    91–117
Burns, Robert, 31
business attire, four categories of,
    66–67
business card exchange, 174–176
business cocktail parties, 171–178
business lunch and dinner, 178–181
business protocol savvy (etiquette),
    165–183
    alcoholic consumption and,
      178–179
    business card exchange and,
      174–176
    business lunch and dinner,
      178–181
    cell phone use and, 178, 181

complimenting others and
    receiving compliments,
    170–171
conversation and, 169, 172–174,
    174, 179–180
decorum in, 166
diplomacy in, 169
discernment in, 166
e-mail and, 181–182
etiquette for every day in,
    167–171
honoring commitments, 168
ice breaking in, 172–174
integrity and authenticity in, 171
introduction skills and, 169, 176
leaving a gathering, 177–178
listening skills in, 169–170
manners and, 166
names and, remembering,
    176–177
netiquette and, 181–183
politeness in, 168, 170
punctuality in, 168, 178
socializing and, 171–181
table manners and, 180–181
thank-you notes and, 170
voice mail and, 182–183

C

career change, 3, 44–45
    pioneer spirit in, 203–208
Carter, Jimmy, 88
casual dress, 64, 67
celebrating success, 208
cell phone use, 178, 181
Center for Nonverbal Studies, 86
character and contribution, 5–6
character/contribution grid, 5–6, **6**
cheerleader, 23, 25

chief knowledge officers
(CKOs), 92
chief learning officers (CLOs), 92
Chopra, Deepak, 94
clients, 1
Clinton, Bill, 87
closed/back and closed/forward
body postures, 83
coaches and mentors, 17, 208
comfort zones, rapport and, 95–96
commonality connection in
presentations, 122
communication skills (*See also*
gender talk; presentations),
3, 29
"connecting" with others, 97–98
fear of speaking and, 120,
135–137
first impression and, 55–56
gender differences in, 147–163
host vs. guest behavior in,
112–117, 139–140
listening skills and, 105–107,
187–188
mixed messages, 55
paralanguage and, 55–56
rapport and, 94–97, 107, **107**
silent language or nonverbal
communication in, 71–89
tell mode vs. share mode in,
130–131
vocal cues, 56–57
word pictures in, 134–135
complimenting others and receiving
compliments, 170–171
confidence and savvy (*See*
appearance, dress), 3, 51,
196–197
confronting others, 109–110

"connecting" with others, 97–98
conscious vs. unconscious,
127–128, **127**
conscious connection with others,
127–128, **127**
consistency of appearance, 62–63
contacts database for
networking, 103
content of presentation, vs.
context, 125–127
context of presentation, 125–127
contribution, 5–6
conversation, 169, 172–174, **174**
etiquette and protocol in,
179–180
gender differences in
communication and, 157–159
corporate casual attire, 66–67
corporate formal attire, 66
Coutu, Diane L., 192, 195
Covey, Stephen, 6
creativity and innovation, 3, 26–27
Creighton University School of
Medicine, 58
criticism, gender differences in
communication and, 153–156
crowd control, in presentations,
142–144
customer service, 3
cutbacks, 12

D

decorum, 166
defensive behavior, nonverbal
communication and, 78
defining your purpose (*See* goal
setting)
delegation, 43
diplomacy, 169

discernment, 166
diversions, 46–47
doing what you love, 200–201
Dole, Bob, 87
dominator personalities, 23, 25–26
Donne, John, quotation by, 185
downsizing, 12
dress (*See* appearance, dress)

E

economic impact, 7
e-mail etiquette, 181–183
emotion, in presentation, 127–128
emotional expression, gender
    differences in communication
    and, 158–159
emotional personality, 29–30
etiquette toolkit, 168–171
etiquette, 167–171
expectancy theory, 58
expectation, power of, 58–59
expectations of others, during
    presentations, 120
experience, 2
expert reputation, 41–44, **43**
expressions (*See* facial expression)
external evaluation (*See* feedback)
extroverts, 104–105
eye contact, 85–87
  hourglass concept in eye contact,
    140, **141**
  presentations and, 124–125, 140

F

facial expression, 87–88
  gender differences in
    communication and,
    152–153, **153**
fact vs. emotion, in presentation,
    127–128
failures as opportunities, 208

false accusations, handling,
    108–109
fear of speaking, 120, 135–137
feedback (*See also* market
    research), 30–33, 188
finding meaning in life, work,
    189–191
first impressions, 53–58, 59
  "bad face day" and, 145–146
  elements of, 55–58
  importance of, 53–54
  job interview research on, 53–55
  mixed message in, 55
  paralanguage and, 55–56
  presence in, 57
  visual impact in, 57, **58**
fixing a reputation, 33–34
focusing on single message in
    presentations, 128–130
focusing on success, 37–39

G

Gates, Bill, image and, 61–62
gender talk, differences in
    communication, 147–163
  aggressive vs. passive behaviors
    in, 160–161
  children and development of,
    148–150
  communication styles and,
    151–152
  conversations and, 157–159
  criticism and, 153–156
  emotional expression and,
    158–159
  importance of, 148, **149**
  job loss and, 150
  learning from the other gender
    in, 162–163
  nonverbal communication and,
    152–153, **152**, **153**

"one up, one down" concept in, 156–157
   relationship building in, 149–150
   socializing and, 161–162
   stereotypes in, 159–160
   taking credit, 156–157
gestures, 53, 140–142
gifts, 11
Givens, David B., 86
goal setting, 4–5, 8–10, 197, 208
   legacy of success, 13–14
Goodall, Jane, 190
grace under fire, 108
gratitude, 193–196, 208
Gray, James, 131
Gray, John, 158
Great Political Wit, 87
guest behavior, 112–117, 139–140

H

happiness, 9
Harvard Business Review, 149, 192
Harvard Law School, 121
Harvard University, 53
head position, in nonverbal communication, 88
hearing vs. listening, 105
hermit, 24, 29
heroes, 7
hidden job market, 91–92
highlighting key points in presentations, 124
homework for presentations, 123–124
honoring commitments, 168
host vs. guest behavior, 112–117, 139–140
hourglass concept in eye contact, 140, **141**
How Resilience Works, 195
how, in mission statement, 11

human capital, 3
humanity, inspirational quotient (IQ) and, 197–198
humility as a virtue, 198, 208

I

ice breaking, 172–174
image (*See also* appearance, dress; first impressions), 51–58, 61–62, 92
   makeovers of, 67–69
   statement made by appearance and, 65–66
impact, 191
   presentations and, 125
impressions, 4–5
inspirational quotient (IQ), 185–201
   attitude of service in, 186–189
   being human and, 197–198
   "bricolage" and, 195
   doing what you love, 200–201
   finding meaning and, 189–191
   gratitude and, 193–196
   priorities and tradeoffs in, 199
   resiliency circle in, 194
   resiliency in life and, 191–196
   self-confidence and, 196–197
   state of being and optimism in, 197
integrity and authenticity, 3, 171
intellectual property and talent, 35–50, 92
   assessment in, 48
   diversions and vocations in, 46–47
   endless loop trap, 37–38, **38**
   focusing on success, 37–39
   power and, personal vs. title, 45–46
   rediscovering, 37–39

intellectual property and
talent (*continued*)
reputation as an expert,
41–44, **43**
roadblocks and, 48–49
specialization and, 47–48
strength and weakness
assessment in, 39–41, **39**
switching tracks or career
changes and, 44–45
talents, skills, expertise in, 36,
38–39
unique abilities and natural
talents in, 39–41
vision in, 48
wisdom in, 36
internal assessment, 23–30
cheerleader vs. lone gun, 23, 25
dominator vs. peacemaker, 23,
25–26
hermit vs. team player in, 24, 29
Myers-Briggs Type Indicator
for, 23
personality traits in, 24–25
qualities and traits in, 23–24
reactive v. Teflon in, 24, 29–30
strengths and weaknesses in, 24
tools for, 23
trailblazer vs. traditionalist in,
24, 26–27
wallflower vs. live wire in, 24,
27–28
wing it vs. plan it in, 24, 28
Internet and netiquette, 181–183
interpersonal skills, 3, 7, 26, 31,
107–112, 198
accepting responsibility in,
110–111
confronting others and, 109–110
false accusations and, handling,
108–109
grace under fire in, 108

host vs. guest behavior in,
112–117, 139–140
"red flag" phrases in, 110
interruptions
controlling the crowd during
presentations, 142–144
gender differences in
communication and, 151
intimidation, 2–3
introduction skills, 169, 176
introverts, 104–105
"ivory tower" work habits, 29

J

job descriptions, 12–13
job interviews
consistency of appearance and,
62–63
first impressions and, 53
looking the part and, 63–65
job loss, gender differences in
communication and, 150
job market, hidden, 91–92

K

Keller, Helen, 9
key points in presentations, 124
King Solomon, 36
Kuczma, Linda, 35
Kushel, Gerald, 9–10

L

leadership, 3, 43, 99
leaving a gathering, 177–178
legacy concept, 3, 4–5, 17–18, 208
beginning with the end in
mind, 6–8
goal setting for, 13–14
life rafts and networking, 93–94
likeability factor, 20–23, **21**

Lipkin, Mike, 200–201
listening skills, 105–107, 169–170, 187–188
live-wire personality, 24, 27–28
lone-gun personality, 23, 25
looking the part, 63–65

M

management, 1
manners and etiquette, 166
market research, 23, 30–31
marketing yourself, 92
master craftsmen, 48
meaning and purpose, 7
meetings, 102, 123–125
Mehrabian, Albert, 55
memorability (*See* legacy)
Men Are from Mars, Women Are from Venus, 158
mentors (*See* coaches and mentors)
messenger of your mission, you as, 19–20
middle casual attire, 67
mission statement, 1–18, 15, 208
    messenger of, you as, 19–20
    power of, 12–14
mixed message, in first impression, 55
Mount Sinai Hospital, 59
"my department" syndrome, 101
Myers-Briggs Type Indicator, 23

N

names, remembering, 176–177
netiquette, 181–183
networking (*See also* communication skills; interpersonal skills), 7, 91–117
    building your life raft ahead of time using, 93–94
    "connecting" with others, 97–98, 97
    contacts database for, 103
    hidden job market and, 91–92
    host vs. guest behavior in, 112–117
    interpersonal skills and, 107–112
    introverts and extroverts in, 104–105
    listening skills and, 105–107
    marketing yourself and, 92
    new employees and, 101
    rapport and, 94–97, 107, **107**
    socializing and, 100–103
    tips for, **104**
    visibility in, 98–104
new employees and networking, 101
New Yorker, 53
nonverbal communication (*See* silent language or nonverbal communication)
Nonverbal Dictionary of Gestures, Signs, and Body Language Cues, The, 86

O

"one up, one down" concept, gender differences in communication and, 156–157
open/forward and open/back body postures, 82
opening remarks or "hook" for presentations, 129–130
opportunities, 42–43
optimists, 197
ordering meals, 179
outplacement, 12
over- vs. underdressing, 63–64

P

paralanguage, 55–56
parties, 171–178
passive behaviors, gender
    differences in communication
    and, 160–161
peacemaker personality, 23, 25–26
peers, 1
"people skills" (*See* interpersonal
    skills)
perceptions vs. reality, 2
perfectionist syndrome, 119–120
performance, 3
personal comfort zones, rapport
    and, 95–96
personal lives vs. work, 9
personal mission statement, 1–18
personal power, 45–46
personality, 5, 24–25
    introverts and extroverts in,
        104–105
    "warm" vs. "cold," body
        language and, 88–89, **89**
perspective, 8–9
pioneer spirit in business, 203–208
politeness, 168, 170
positive vs. negative self-image,
    58–59
posture, 84–85
power of mission, 12–14
power of three concept, in
    presentations, 131–132
power, personal vs. title, 45–46
prepaying the bill, 179
presence, 57
    body posture in, 84
presentations, 119–146
    audience for, 121, **121**, 124
    "bad face day" and,
        145–146, 145
    baseball technique in, 140
    commonality connection in, 122
    "connecting" with others in,
        conscious vs. unconscious,
        127–128, **127**
    context vs. content in, 125–127
    delivery of, 124, 126
    expectations of others in, 120
    eye contact in, 124–125, 140
    fact vs. emotion in, 127–128
    fear of speaking and, 120,
        135–137
    focusing on single message in,
        128–130
    gestures during, 140–142
    highlighting key points in, 124
    homework for, 123–124
    host behavior in, 139–140
    hourglass concept in eye contact
        during, 140, **141**
    impact of, 125
    interruptions and controlling the
        crowd in, 142–144
    messing up and muddling
        through, 144–145
    opening remarks or "hook" for,
        129–130
    perfectionist syndrome vs.,
        119–120
    power of three concept in,
        131–132
    preparation for, 137–139
    setting or room for, 137–139
    short presentations and, 123
    staff meetings and, 123–125
    tell mode vs. share mode in,
        130–131
    timing in, 132–133
    visuals in, 133–135
    word pictures in, 134–135
priorities and tradeoffs, 199
protocol (*See* business protocol
    savvy)
punctuality, 168, 178

Q

qualities and traits, 2, 3, 5, 23–24

R

rapport, 107, **107**
  networking and, 94–97
reactive personality, 24, 29–30
"reading" others using nonverbal
      communication, 76–77
"red flag" phrases, 110
relationship building, gender
      differences in communication
      and, 149–150
relaxed casual attire, 67
reputation, 33–34
  "expert," 41–44, **43**
reserved natures, 27–28
resiliency circle, 194
resiliency in life, 191–196
responsibilities, 7–8, 110–111
roadblocks, 48–49
role playing, 148
Roots & Shoots program (Jane
      Goodall), 190

S

S.C. Cooper Sports Medicine
      Clinic, 59
"safety zones" or personal comfort
      zones, 95–96
salespersons, 20
sample mission statement, 11
seating, formal dinners, 179
"selective *See*" doctors, 20
self confidence and self esteem,
      73–76, **74**, 196–197
self-image, 58–59
service to others, 186–189
Settineri, Vince, 193
*Seven Habits of Highly Effective
      People, The*, 6

*Seven Spiritual Laws of Success,
      The*, 94
share mode, presentations and,
      130–131
silent language or nonverbal
      communication, 71–89
  body language and body posture
      in, 81–85
  defensive behavior in, 78
  eye contact in, 85–87
  facial expression in, 87–88
  gender differences in
      communication and, 152–153,
      152, **153**
  gestures, 140–142
  head position in, 88
  listening skills and, 106–107
  perfecting your posture in, 83–85
  posture and, 84
  presence and, 84
  sabotaging yourself with, 79–80
  self confidence and self esteem,
      73–76, **74**
  smiles in, 87–88
  subconscious nature of, 72,
      80–82
  taking a reading using, 76–77
  unlocking and using, 80–82
  "warm" vs. "cold" personalities
      and, 88–89, **89**
  wrong interpretation or reading
      of, 77–79
smiles, 87–88
socializing
  etiquette and protocol in,
      171–181
  gender differences in
      communication and, 161–162
  networking and, 100–103
specialization, 47–48
staff meetings, 123–125
state of being, 197

statement made by appearance,
        65–66
steps to success, 15–18
stereotypes in gender
        communication, 159–160
Strategic Coach, Inc., The, 39
strategy, 15–16, 19–34, 92
    feedback in, 32–33
    fixing a reputation, 33–34
    likeability factor in, 20–23, **21**
    market research in, 30–31
    messenger of your mission in,
        you as, 19–20
    roadblocks in, 49
strength and weakness assessment,
        24, 39–41, **39**
success vs. happiness, 9
    doing what you love, 200–201
    focusing on, 37–39
    goal setting for, 13–14
    steps to, 15–18
Sulewski, Marsha, 60–61
Sullivan, Dan, 39
switching tracks (*See* career
        changes)

T

table manners, 180–181
talents (*See also* intellectual
        property), 2, 3, 5, 8, 11, 36,
        38–41, 92, 208
    reputation as an expert in,
        41–44, **43**
    switching tracks or career
        changes and, 44–45
    unique abilities and natural
        talents in, 39–41
Tannen, Deborah, 148–149, 156
Taylor, Ron, 59
team player, 24, 25, 26, 29, 99
Teflon personality, 24, 29–30

telemarketing, 56–57
telephone skills, vocal cues and,
        56–57
tell mode, presentations and,
        130–131
"temperature reading," using
        nonverbal communication,
        76–77
thank-you notes, 170
time frame, for career customizing,
        16–17
Time magazine, 189
time management, 28
timing, in presentations and,
        132–133
title power, 45–46
Toogood, Granville M., 133
Toronto Globe and Mail, 131
traditionalist personality, 24, 26–27
trailblazer personality, 24, 26–27
transforming yourself, 22
Twelve B's of professional
        appearance, **63**

U

unconscious connection with
        others, 127–128, **127**
unique abilities and natural talents
        in, 39–41
University of Southern California
        (UCLA), 55
University of Toledo, 53
Usheroff Institute, 12

V

values, 3, 5
visibility in networking, 98–104
vision, 15, 48
visual impact, 57, **58**
visuals for presentations, 133–135
vocal cues, 56–57

vocations, 46–47
voice mail, 182–183

W

Wall Street Journal, 64, 92
Wallenstein & Wagner law firm, 35
wallflower personality, 24, 27–28
Wal-Mart, 189–190
Walton, Sam, 189–190
"warm" vs. "cold" personalities,
    nonverbal communication
      and, 88–89, **89**

Wellness Chronicle, 58
what, in mission statement, 11
who, in mission statement, 11
wing it vs. plan it personalities,
    24, 28
wisdom, 36
word pictures, 134–135

Y

Your Personal Best, 200–201

About the Author

Roz Usheroff, principal of The Usheroff Institute, Inc., is a professional speaker, executive coach, and communications and image specialist. Her techniques have proven equally valuable to Fortune 500 executives, sales teams, and employees at all levels. Roz helps her clients to increase their personal power and gain stronger visibility with their customers.

Her extensive corporate client list includes Pfizer, Jergens, Aramark, ACNielsen, Sony, Harlequin Enterprises Limited, Harris Trust and Savings Bank, Manulife Financial, and Johnson & Johnson. Her programs range from presentations before an audience of thousands to small group workshops and one-on-one executive coaching.

Through her intensive work with professionals at every level, Roz is in touch with the realities of today's business environment—including specific challenges facing top executives, mid-level professionals, those starting out on their careers, and others who find themselves suddenly "in transition." Through her experience and expertise, she is able to share what works, what doesn't, and why. Her message is critically important for professionals who want to invest in their career and personal success.

She has delivered her message on national television and radio and in print publications.

For more information on The Usheroff Institute, Inc., see the web site at www.usheroff.com.